MznLnx

Missing Links Exam Preps

Exam Prep for

Matching Supply with Demand: An Introduction to Operations Management

Cachon & Terwiesch, 2nd Edition

The MznLnx Exam Prep is your link from the texbook and lecture to your exams.
The MznLnx Exam Preps are unauthorized and comprehensive reviews of your textbooks.

All material provided by MznLnx and Rico Publications (c) 2010
Textbook publishers and textbook authors do not particpate in or contribute to these reviews.

MznLnx

Rico Publications

Exam Prep for Matching Supply with Demand: An Introduction to Operations Management
2nd Edition
Cachon & Terwiesch

Publisher: Raymond Houge
Assistant Editor: Michael Rouger
Text and Cover Designer: Lisa Buckner
Marketing Manager: Sara Swagger
Project Manager, Editorial Production: Jerry Emerson
Art Director: Vernon Lowerui

Product Manager: Dave Mason
Editorial Assitant: Rachel Guzmanji
Pedagogy: Debra Long
Cover Image: Jim Reed/Getty Images
Text and Cover Printer: City Printing, Inc.
Compositor: Media Mix, Inc.

(c) 2010 Rico Publications

ALL RIGHTS RESERVED. No part of this work covered by the copyright may be reproduced or used in any form or by an means--graphic, electronic, or mechanical, including photocopying, recording, taping, Web distribution, information storage, and retrieval systems, or in any other manner--without the written permission of the publisher.

Printed in the United States
ISBN:

For more information about our products, contact us at:
Dave.Mason@RicoPublications.com

For permission to use material from this text or product, submit a request online to:
Dave.Mason@RicoPublications.com

Contents

CHAPTER 1
The Process View of the Organization — 1

CHAPTER 2
Understanding the Supply Process: Evaluating Process Capacity — 7

CHAPTER 3
Estimating and Reducing Labor Costs — 8

CHAPTER 4
The Link between Operations and Finance — 10

CHAPTER 5
Batching and Other Flow Interruptions — 14

CHAPTER 6
Variability and Its Impact on Process Performance: Waiting Time Problems — 17

CHAPTER 7
The Impact of Variability on Process Performance: Throughput Losses — 25

CHAPTER 8
Quality Management, Statistical Process Control, and Six-Sigma Capability — 28

CHAPTER 9
Lean Operations and the Toyota Production System — 33

CHAPTER 10
Betting on Uncertain Demand: The Newsvendor Model — 40

CHAPTER 11
Assemble-to-Order, Make-to-Order, and Quick Response with Reactive Capacity — 46

CHAPTER 12
Service Levels and Lead Times in Supply Chains: The Order-up-to Inventory Model — 49

CHAPTER 13
Risk-Pooling Strategies to Reduce and Hedge Uncertainty — 57

CHAPTER 14
Revenue Management with Capacity Controls — 62

CHAPTER 15
Supply Chain Coordination — 65

ANSWER KEY — 76

TO THE STUDENT

COMPREHENSIVE

The *MznLnx* Exam Prep series is designed to help you pass your exams. Editors at MznLnx review your textbooks and then prepare these practice exams to help you master the textbook material. Unlike study guides, workbooks, and practice tests provided by the texbook publisher and textbook authors, *MznLnx* gives you **all** of the material in each chapter in exam form, not just samples, so you can be sure to nail your exam.

MECHANICAL

The MznLnx Exam Prep series creates exams that will help you learn the subject matter as well as test you on your understanding. Each question is designed to help you master the concept. Just working through the exams, you gain an understanding of the subject--its a simple mechanical process that produces success.

INTEGRATED STUDY GUIDE AND REVIEW

MznLnx is not just a set of exams designed to test you, its also a comprehensive review of the subject content. Each exam question is also a review of the concept, making sure that you will get the answer correct without having to go to other sources of material. You learn as you go! Its the easiest way to pass an exam.

HUMOR

Studying can be tedious and dry. MznLnx's instructional design includes moderate humor within the exam questions on occassion, to break the tedium and revitalize the brain

Chapter 1. The Process View of the Organization

1. _____ refers to the movement of cash into or out of a business or financial product. It is usually measured during a specified, finite period of time. Measurement of _____ can be used

   - to determine a project's rate of return or value. The time of _____s into and out of projects are used as inputs in financial models such as internal rate of return, and net present value.
   - to determine problems with a business's liquidity. Being profitable does not necessarily mean being liquid. A company can fail because of a shortage of cash, even while profitable.
   - as an alternate measure of a business's profits when it is believed that accrual accounting concepts do not represent economic realities. For example, a company may be notionally profitable but generating little operational cash (as may be the case for a company that barters its products rather than selling for cash.) In such a case, the company may be deriving additional operating cash by issuing shares evaluating default risk, re-investment requirements, etc.

   _____ is a generic term used differently depending on the context. It may be defined by users for their own purposes.

   a. Sweat equity
   b. Gross profit
   c. Gross profit margin
   d. Cash flow

2. _____ is the discipline of planning, organizing and managing resources to bring about the successful completion of specific project goals and objectives. It is often closely related to and sometimes conflated with Program management.

   A project is a finite endeavor--having specific start and completion dates--undertaken to meet particular goals and objectives, usually to bring about beneficial change or added value.

   a. Work package
   b. Project management
   c. Project engineer
   d. Precedence diagram

3. In decision theory and estimation theory, the _____ of an estimator, $\hat{\theta}$, of an unknown parameter of the distribution, θ, is the expected value of the loss function

$$R(\theta, \hat{\theta}) = \mathbb{E}_\theta L(\theta, \hat{\theta}) = \int L(\theta, \hat{\theta}) \, dP_\theta.$$

where dP_θ is a probability measure parametrized by θ.

- For a scalar parameter θ and a quadratic loss function,

$$L(\theta, \hat{\theta}) = (\theta - \hat{\theta})^2$$

the _____ function becomes the mean squared error of the estimate,

$$R(\theta, \hat{\theta}) = E_\theta(\theta - \hat{\theta})^2$$

- In density estimation, the unknown parameter is probability density itself. The loss function is typically chosen to be a norm in an appropriate function space. For example, for L^2 norm,

$$L(f, \hat{f}) = \|f - \hat{f}\|_2^2$$

the _____ function becomes the mean integrated squared error

$$R(f, \hat{f}) = E\|f - \hat{f}\|^2$$

a. Risk aversion
b. Financial modeling
c. Linear model
d. Risk

4. In economics, business, retail, and accounting, a _____ is the value of money that has been used up to produce something, and hence is not available for use anymore. In economics, a _____ is an alternative that is given up as a result of a decision. In business, the _____ may be one of acquisition, in which case the amount of money expended to acquire it is counted as _____.
a. Cost allocation
b. Fixed costs
c. Cost overrun
d. Cost

5. In business and accounting, _____s are everything of value that is owned by a person or company. Any property or object of value that one possesses, usually considered as applicable to the payment of one's debts is considered an _____. Simplistically stated, _____s are things of value that can be readily converted into cash.

a. A4e
b. AAAI
c. A Stake in the Outcome
d. Asset

6. In financial accounting, _____ or cost of sales includes the direct costs attributable to the production of the goods sold by a company. This amount includes the materials cost used in creating the goods along with the direct labour costs used to produce the good. It excludes indirect expenses such as distribution costs and sales force costs.
   a. 28-hour day
   b. 1990 Clean Air Act
   c. Reorder point
   d. Cost of goods sold

7. In a human resources context, _____ or labor _____ is the rate at which an employer gains and loses employees. Simple ways to describe it are 'how long employees tend to stay' or 'the rate of traffic through the revolving door.' _____ is measured for individual companies and for their industry as a whole. If an employer is said to have a high _____ relative to its competitors, it means that employees of that company have a shorter average tenure than those of other companies in the same industry.
   a. Continuous
   b. Ten year occupational employment projection
   c. Career portfolios
   d. Turnover

8. The _____ is an equation that equals the cost of goods sold divided by the average inventory. Average inventory equals beginning inventory plus ending inventory divided by 2.

The formula for _____:

The formula for average inventory:

A low turnover rate may point to overstocking, obsolescence, or deficiencies in the product line or marketing effort.

a. Asset turnover
b. A Stake in the Outcome
c. Inventory turnover
d. A4e

9. In business management, _____ is money spent to keep and maintain a stock of goods in storage.

The most obvious _____s include rent for the required space; equipment, materials, and labor to operate the space; insurance; security; interest on money invested in the inventory and space, and other direct expenses. Some stored goods become obsolete before they are sold, reducing their contribution to revenue while having no effect on their _____.

a. Choquet integral
b. Market niche
c. Private placement
d. Holding cost

10. _____, Gross profit margin or Gross Profit Rate can be defined as the amount of contribution to the business enterprise, after paying for direct-fixed and direct-variable unit costs, required to cover overheads (fixed commitments) and provide a buffer for unknown items. It expresses the relationship between gross profit and sales revenue.

It can be expressed in absolute terms:

Gross Profit = Revenue − Cost of Sales

or as the ratio of gross profit to sales revenue, usually in the form of a percentage:

_____ Percentage = (Revenue-Cost of Sales)/Revenue

Cost of Sales includes variable costs and fixed costs directly linked to the product, such as material and labor.

a. 1990 Clean Air Act
b. Gross margin
c. Profit maximization
d. Profit margin

11. _____, in microeconomics, are the cost advantages that a business obtains due to expansion. They are factors that cause a producer's average cost per unit to fall as scale is increased. _____ is a long run concept and refers to reductions in unit cost as the size of a facility, or scale, increases.

Chapter 1. The Process View of the Organization 5

a. A Stake in the Outcome
b. A4e
c. Economies of scope
d. Economies of scale

12. Network externalities resemble economies of scale, but they are not considered such because they are a function of the number of users of a good or service in an industry, not of the production efficiency within a business. _____ are only considered examples of network externalities if they are driven by demand side economies.

Formally, a production function $\boxed{\times}$> is defined to have:

- constant returns to scale if (for any constant a greater than or equal to 0) $\boxed{\times}$>
- increasing returns to scale if (for any constant a greater than 1) $\boxed{\times}$>
- decreasing returns to scale if (for any constant a greater than 1) $\boxed{\times}$>

where K and L are factors of production, capital and labour, respectively.

As an example, the Cobb-Douglas functional form has constant returns to scale when the sum of the exponents adds up to one.

a. AAAI
b. A Stake in the Outcome
c. A4e
d. Economies of scale external to the firm

13. In economics, _____ is the desire to own something and the ability to pay for it. The term _____ signifies the ability or the willingness to buy a particular commodity at a given point of time.
a. 1990 Clean Air Act
b. 33 Strategies of War
c. 28-hour day
d. Demand

14. In statistics, many time series exhibit cyclic variation known as _____, periodic variation, or periodic fluctuations. This variation can be either regular or semiregular.

For example, retail sales tend to peak for the Christmas season and then decline after the holidays.

a. 28-hour day
b. 1990 Clean Air Act
c. 33 Strategies of War
d. Seasonality

Chapter 2. Understanding the Supply Process: Evaluating Process Capacity 7

1. A _____ is a computer program typically used to provide some form of artificial intelligence, which consists primarily of a set of rules about behavior. These rules, termed productions, are a basic representation found useful in AI planning, expert systems and action selection. A _____ provides the mechanism necessary to execute productions in order to achieve some goal for the system.
   a. 28-hour day
   b. 1990 Clean Air Act
   c. 33 Strategies of War
   d. Production System

2. In queueing theory, _____ is the proportion of the system's resources which is used by the traffic which arrives at it. It should be strictly less than one for the system to function well. It is usually represented by the symbol ρ.
   a. AAAI
   b. Utilization
   c. A Stake in the Outcome
   d. A4e

Chapter 3. Estimating and Reducing Labor Costs

1. _____ in manufacturing refers to processes that occur later on in a production sequence or production line.

Viewing a company 'from order to cash' might have high-level processes such as Marketing, Sales, Order Entry, Manufacturing, Packaging, Shipping, Invoicing. Each of these could be deconstructed into many sub-processes and supporting processes.

   a. Downstream
   b. Science Learning Centre
   c. Genbutsu
   d. Probability-generating function

2. In economics, _____ is the desire to own something and the ability to pay for it. The term _____ signifies the ability or the willingness to buy a particular commodity at a given point of time.
   a. Demand
   b. 28-hour day
   c. 33 Strategies of War
   d. 1990 Clean Air Act

3. In economics, business, retail, and accounting, a _____ is the value of money that has been used up to produce something, and hence is not available for use anymore. In economics, a _____ is an alternative that is given up as a result of a decision. In business, the _____ may be one of acquisition, in which case the amount of money expended to acquire it is counted as _____.
   a. Cost overrun
   b. Cost
   c. Cost allocation
   d. Fixed costs

4. In queueing theory, _____ is the proportion of the system's resources which is used by the traffic which arrives at it. It should be strictly less than one for the system to function well. It is usually represented by the symbol ρ.
   a. A Stake in the Outcome
   b. A4e
   c. AAAI
   d. Utilization

5. _____ is a term originating in military organization theory, but now used more commonly in business management, particularly human resource management. _____ refers to the number of subordinates a supervisor has.

In the hierarchical business organization of the past it was not uncommon to see average spans of 1 to 10 or even less. That is, one manager supervised ten employees on average.

Chapter 3. Estimating and Reducing Labor Costs

a. Span of control
b. Mentoring
c. Senior management
d. CIFMS

6. _____ is one of the managerial functions like planning, organizing, staffing and directing. It is an important function because it helps to check the errors and to take the corrective action so that deviation from standards are minimized and stated goals of the organization are achieved in desired manner. According to modern concepts, _____ is a foreseeing action whereas earlier concept of _____ was used only when errors were detected. _____ in management means setting standards, measuring actual performance and taking corrective action.

a. Turnover
b. Control
c. Schedule of reinforcement
d. Decision tree pruning

Chapter 4. The Link between Operations and Finance

1. In decision theory and estimation theory, the _____ of an estimator, $\hat{\theta}$, of an unknown parameter of the distribution, θ, is the expected value of the loss function

$$R(\theta, \hat{\theta}) = \mathbb{E}_\theta L(\theta, \hat{\theta}) = \int L(\theta, \hat{\theta})\, dP_\theta.$$

where dP_θ is a probability measure parametrized by θ.

- For a scalar parameter θ and a quadratic loss function,

$$L(\theta, \hat{\theta}) = (\theta - \hat{\theta})^2$$

the _____ function becomes the mean squared error of the estimate,

$$R(\theta, \hat{\theta}) = E_\theta (\theta - \hat{\theta})^2$$

- In density estimation, the unknown parameter is probability density itself. The loss function is typically chosen to be a norm in an appropriate function space. For example, for L^2 norm,

$$L(f, \hat{f}) = \|f - \hat{f}\|_2^2$$

the _____ function becomes the mean integrated squared error

$$R(f, \hat{f}) = E\|f - \hat{f}\|^2$$

a. Risk aversion
b. Linear model
c. Financial modeling
d. Risk

2. In a human resources context, _____ or labor _____ is the rate at which an employer gains and loses employees. Simple ways to describe it are 'how long employees tend to stay' or 'the rate of traffic through the revolving door.' _____ is measured for individual companies and for their industry as a whole. If an employer is said to have a high _____ relative to its competitors, it means that employees of that company have a shorter average tenure than those of other companies in the same industry.

a. Career portfolios
b. Continuous
c. Ten year occupational employment projection
d. Turnover

3. The _____ is an equation that equals the cost of goods sold divided by the average inventory. Average inventory equals beginning inventory plus ending inventory divided by 2.

The formula for _____:

The formula for average inventory:

A low turnover rate may point to overstocking, obsolescence, or deficiencies in the product line or marketing effort.

a. A4e
b. Asset turnover
c. Inventory turnover
d. A Stake in the Outcome

4. _____ represents the total cash investment that shareholders and debtholders have made in a company. There are two different but completely equivalent methods for calculating _____. The operating approach is calculated as:

_____ = Operating Net Working Capital + Net PP'E + Capitalized Operating Leases + Other Operating Assets + Operating Intangibles - Other Operating Liabilities - Cumulative Adjustment for Amortization of R'D

Equivalently, the financing approach is calculated as:

In symbols:

$$K = D + E - M$$

_____ is used in several important measurements of financial performance, including return on _____, economic value added, and free cash flow.

Chapter 4. The Link between Operations and Finance

　　a. AAAI
　　b. A Stake in the Outcome
　　c. A4e
　　d. Invested capital

5. In business and accounting, _____s are everything of value that is owned by a person or company. Any property or object of value that one possesses, usually considered as applicable to the payment of one's debts is considered an _____. Simplistically stated, _____s are things of value that can be readily converted into cash.

　　a. AAAI
　　b. A4e
　　c. Asset
　　d. A Stake in the Outcome

6. In economics, business, retail, and accounting, a _____ is the value of money that has been used up to produce something, and hence is not available for use anymore. In economics, a _____ is an alternative that is given up as a result of a decision. In business, the _____ may be one of acquisition, in which case the amount of money expended to acquire it is counted as _____.

　　a. Cost overrun
　　b. Cost allocation
　　c. Fixed costs
　　d. Cost

7. _____s are expenses that change in proportion to the activity of a business. In other words, _____ is the sum of marginal costs. It can also be considered normal costs.

　　a. Variable cost
　　b. Cost overrun
　　c. Fixed costs
　　d. Cost accounting

8. In economics, _____ are business expenses that are not dependent on the activities of the business They tend to be time-related, such as salaries or rents being paid per month. This is in contrast to variable costs, which are volume-related (and are paid per quantity.)

In management accounting, _____ are defined as expenses that do not change in proportion to the activity of a business, within the relevant period or scale of production.

Chapter 4. The Link between Operations and Finance

a. Transaction cost
b. Cost of quality
c. Cost allocation
d. Fixed costs

9. _____ plant, and equipment, is a term used in accountancy for assets and property which cannot easily be converted into cash. This can be compared with current assets such as cash or bank accounts, which are described as liquid assets. In most cases, only tangible assets are referred to as fixed.

a. 1990 Clean Air Act
b. Fixed asset
c. 28-hour day
d. 33 Strategies of War

10. _____ is the process of understanding, anticipating and influencing consumer behavior in order to maximize revenue or profits from a fixed, perishable resource This process was first discovered by Dr. Matt H. Keller. The challenge is to sell the right resources to the right customer at the right time for the right price.

a. Business networking
b. Gap analysis
c. Business model design
d. Yield management

11. _____ refers to metrics and measures of output from production processes, per unit of input. Labor _____, for example, is typically measured as a ratio of output per labor-hour, an input. _____ may be conceived of as a metrics of the technical or engineering efficiency of production.

a. Master production schedule
b. Value engineering
c. Productivity
d. Remanufacturing

Chapter 5. Batching and Other Flow Interruptions

1. The metastability in flip-flops can be avoided by ensuring that the data and control inputs are held valid and constant for specified periods before and after the clock pulse, called the _____ and the hold time (t_h) respectively. These times are specified in the data sheet for the device, and are typically between a few nanoseconds and a few hundred picoseconds for modern devices.

    Unfortunately, it is not always possible to meet the setup and hold criteria, because the flip-flop may be connected to a real-time signal that could change at any time, outside the control of the designer.

    a. 33 Strategies of War
    b. 28-hour day
    c. 1990 Clean Air Act
    d. Setup time

2. In economics, business, retail, and accounting, a _____ is the value of money that has been used up to produce something, and hence is not available for use anymore. In economics, a _____ is an alternative that is given up as a result of a decision. In business, the _____ may be one of acquisition, in which case the amount of money expended to acquire it is counted as _____.

    a. Cost allocation
    b. Fixed costs
    c. Cost overrun
    d. Cost

3. _____ or economic opportunity loss is the value of the next best alternative forgone as the result of making a decision. _____ analysis is an important part of a company's decision-making processes but is not treated as an actual cost in any financial statement. The next best thing that a person can engage in is referred to as the _____ of doing the best thing and ignoring the next best thing to be done.

    a. A Stake in the Outcome
    b. AAAI
    c. A4e
    d. Opportunity cost

4. _____, in microeconomics, are the cost advantages that a business obtains due to expansion. They are factors that cause a producer's average cost per unit to fall as scale is increased. _____ is a long run concept and refers to reductions in unit cost as the size of a facility, or scale, increases.

    a. A Stake in the Outcome
    b. Economies of scope
    c. A4e
    d. Economies of scale

Chapter 5. Batching and Other Flow Interruptions

5. Network externalities resemble economies of scale, but they are not considered such because they are a function of the number of users of a good or service in an industry, not of the production efficiency within a business. _____ are only considered examples of network externalities if they are driven by demand side economies.

Formally, a production function F is defined to have:

- constant returns to scale if (for any constant a greater than or equal to 0) $F(aK, aL) = aF(K, L)$
- increasing returns to scale if (for any constant a greater than 1) $F(aK, aL) > aF(K, L)$
- decreasing returns to scale if (for any constant a greater than 1) $F(aK, aL) < aF(K, L)$

where K and L are factors of production, capital and labour, respectively.

As an example, the Cobb-Douglas functional form has constant returns to scale when the sum of the exponents adds up to one.

a. AAAI
b. A4e
c. A Stake in the Outcome
d. Economies of scale external to the firm

6. _____ is the state of being which occurs when a person, object, or service is no longer wanted even though it may still be in good working order. _____ frequently occurs because a replacement has become available that is superior in one or more aspects. Videotapes making way for DVDs

Technical _____ may occur when a new product or technology supersedes the old, and it becomes preferred to utilize the new technology in place of the old.

a. A Stake in the Outcome
b. Obsolescence
c. AAAI
d. A4e

7. _____ is the level of inventory that minimizes the total inventory holding costs and ordering costs. The framework used to determine this order quantity is also known as Wilson _____ Model. The model was developed by F. W. Harris in 1913.

Chapter 5. Batching and Other Flow Interruptions

   a. Anti-leadership
   b. Economic order quantity
   c. Event management
   d. Effective executive

8. In probability theory, a probability distribution is called _____ if its cumulative distribution function is _____. This is equivalent to saying that for random variables X with the distribution in question, Pr[X = a] = 0 for all real numbers a, i.e.: the probability that X attains the value a is zero, for any number a. If the distribution of X is _____ then X is called a _____ random variable.
   a. Decision tree pruning
   b. Pay Band
   c. Connectionist expert systems
   d. Continuous

9. _____ is one of the many lean production methods for reducing waste in a manufacturing process. It provides a rapid and efficient way of converting a manufacturing process from running the current product to running the next product. This rapid changeover is key to reducing production lot sizes and thereby improving flow ' href='/wiki/Mura_'>Mura) The phrase 'single minute' does not mean that all changeovers and startups should take only one minute, but that they should take less than 10 minutes (in other words, 'single digit minute'.)
   a. Process capability
   b. Statistical process control
   c. Quality control
   d. Single Minute Exchange of Die

10. The _____ of an edge is $c_f(u,v) = c(u,v) - f(u,v)$. This defines a residual network denoted $G_f(V, E_f)$, giving the amount of available capacity. See that there can be an edge from u to v in the residual network, even though there is no edge from u to v in the original network.
   a. Residual capacity
   b. 1990 Clean Air Act
   c. 28-hour day
   d. 33 Strategies of War

Chapter 6. Variability and Its Impact on Process Performance: Waiting Time Problems

1. In economics, _____ is the desire to own something and the ability to pay for it. The term _____ signifies the ability or the willingness to buy a particular commodity at a given point of time.
    a. 33 Strategies of War
    b. 1990 Clean Air Act
    c. 28-hour day
    d. Demand

2. In probability theory and statistics, _____ is a measure of the variability or dispersion of a population, a data set, or a probability distribution. A low _____ indicates that the data points tend to be very close to the same value (the mean), while high _____ indicates that the data are 'spread out' over a large range of values.

    For example, the average height for adult men in the United States is about 70 inches (178 cm), with a _____ of around 3 in (8 cm.)

    a. Frequency distribution
    b. Normal distribution
    c. Failure rate
    d. Standard deviation

3. _____ is one of the four elements of marketing mix. An organization or set of organizations (go-betweens) involved in the process of making a product or service available for use or consumption by a consumer or business user.

    The other three parts of the marketing mix are product, pricing, and promotion.

    a. Distribution
    b. Matching theory
    c. Job creation programs
    d. Missing completely at random

4. In probability theory and statistics, the _____ is a normalized measure of dispersion of a probability distribution. It is defined as the ratio of the standard deviation σ to the mean μ:

$$c_v = \frac{\sigma}{\mu}$$

This is only defined for non-zero mean, and is most useful for variables that are always positive. It is also known as unitized risk.

18 *Chapter 6. Variability and Its Impact on Process Performance: Waiting Time Problems*

   a. Failure rate
   b. Frequency distribution
   c. Control chart
   d. Coefficient of variation

5. In statistics, _____ is:

   - the arithmetic _____
   - the expected value of a random variable, which is also called the population _____.

It is sometimes stated that the '_____' _____s average. This is incorrect if '_____' is taken in the specific sense of 'arithmetic _____' as there are different types of averages: the _____, median, and mode. Other simple statistical analyses use measures of spread, such as range, interquartile range, or standard deviation. For a real-valued random variable X, the _____ is the expectation of X. Note that not every probability distribution has a defined _____; see the Cauchy distribution for an example.

   a. Statistical inference
   b. Mean
   c. Control chart
   d. Correlation

6. In mathematics, _____ are used in the study of chance and probability. They were developed to assist in the analysis of games of chance, stochastic events, and the results of scientific experiments by capturing only the mathematical properties necessary to answer probabilistic questions. Further formalizations have firmly grounded the entity in the theoretical domains of mathematics by making use of measure theory.
   a. Median
   b. Correlation
   c. Time series
   d. Random variables

7. In probability theory and statistics, the _____s are a class of continuous probability distributions. They describe the times between events in a Poisson process, i.e. a process in which events occur continuously and independently at a constant average rate.

The probability density function (pdf) of an _____ is

>

Here >λ > 0 is the parameter of the distribution, often called the rate parameter.

Chapter 6. Variability and Its Impact on Process Performance: Waiting Time Problems

a. A Stake in the Outcome
b. Exponential distribution
c. A4e
d. AAAI

8. In statistics, many time series exhibit cyclic variation known as _____, periodic variation, or periodic fluctuations. This variation can be either regular or semiregular.

For example, retail sales tend to peak for the Christmas season and then decline after the holidays.

a. 1990 Clean Air Act
b. Seasonality
c. 28-hour day
d. 33 Strategies of War

9. In probability theory and statistics, the _____ or just distribution function, completely describes the probability distribution of a real-valued random variable X. For every real number x, the _____ of X is given by

where the right-hand side represents the probability that the random variable X takes on a value less than or equal to x. The probability that X lies in the interval (a, b] is therefore $F_X(b) >- F_X(a)$ if a < b.

If treating several random variables X, Y, ...

a. 33 Strategies of War
b. 1990 Clean Air Act
c. 28-hour day
d. Cumulative distribution function

10. In statistics, a _____ is a graphical display of tabulated frequencies, shown as bars. It shows what proportion of cases fall into each of several categories: it is a form of data binning. The categories are usually specified as non-overlapping intervals of some variable.

Chapter 6. Variability and Its Impact on Process Performance: Waiting Time Problems

a. Histogram
b. Statistics
c. Standard deviation
d. Correlation

11. _____ plant, and equipment, is a term used in accountancy for assets and property which cannot easily be converted into cash. This can be compared with current assets such as cash or bank accounts, which are described as liquid assets. In most cases, only tangible assets are referred to as fixed.

a. Fixed asset
b. 33 Strategies of War
c. 1990 Clean Air Act
d. 28-hour day

12. _____ is an advertisement in which a particular product specifically mentions a competitor by name for the express purpose of showing why the competitor is inferior to the product naming it.

This should not be confused with parody advertisements, where a fictional product is being advertised for the purpose of poking fun at the particular advertisement, nor should it be confused with the use of a coined brand name for the purpose of comparing the product without actually naming an actual competitor. ('Wikipedia tastes better and is less filling than the Encyclopedia Galactica.')

In the 1980s, during what has been referred to as the cola wars, soft-drink manufacturer Pepsi ran a series of advertisements where people, caught on hidden camera, in a blind taste test, chose Pepsi over rival Coca-Cola.

a. 33 Strategies of War
b. 28-hour day
c. 1990 Clean Air Act
d. Comparative advertising

13. _____ measures the performance of a system. Certain goals are defined and the _____ gives the percentage to which they should be achieved.

Examples

- Percentage of calls answered in a call center.
- Percentage of customers waiting less than a given fixed time.
- Percentage of customers that do not experience a stock out.

Chapter 6. Variability and Its Impact on Process Performance: Waiting Time Problems

_____ is used in supply chain management and in inventory management to measure the performance of inventory systems.

Under stochastic conditions it is unavoidable that in some periods the inventory on hand is not sufficient to deliver the complete demand and, as a consequence, that part of the demand is filled only after an inventory-related waiting time.

a. 33 Strategies of War
b. 1990 Clean Air Act
c. 28-hour day
d. Service level

14. In economics, business, retail, and accounting, a _____ is the value of money that has been used up to produce something, and hence is not available for use anymore. In economics, a _____ is an alternative that is given up as a result of a decision. In business, the _____ may be one of acquisition, in which case the amount of money expended to acquire it is counted as _____.

a. Cost allocation
b. Cost overrun
c. Fixed costs
d. Cost

15. _____, in microeconomics, are the cost advantages that a business obtains due to expansion. They are factors that cause a producer's average cost per unit to fall as scale is increased. _____ is a long run concept and refers to reductions in unit cost as the size of a facility, or scale, increases.

a. A4e
b. A Stake in the Outcome
c. Economies of scope
d. Economies of scale

16. In decision theory and estimation theory, the _____ of an estimator, $\hat{\theta}$, of an unknown parameter of the distribution, θ, is the expected value of the loss function

$$R(\theta, \hat{\theta}) = \mathbb{E}_\theta L(\theta, \hat{\theta}) = \int L(\theta, \hat{\theta})\, dP_\theta.$$

where dP_θ is a probability measure parametrized by θ.

- For a scalar parameter θ and a quadratic loss function,

$$L(\theta, \hat{\theta}) = (\theta - \hat{\theta})^2$$

the _____ function becomes the mean squared error of the estimate,

$$R(\theta, \hat{\theta}) = E_\theta(\theta - \hat{\theta})^2$$

- In density estimation, the unknown parameter is probability density itself. The loss function is typically chosen to be a norm in an appropriate function space. For example, for L^2 norm,

$$L(f, \hat{f}) = \|f - \hat{f}\|_2^2$$

the _____ function becomes the mean integrated squared error

$$R(f, \hat{f}) = E\|f - \hat{f}\|^2$$

a. Risk aversion
b. Linear model
c. Risk
d. Financial modeling

17. Network externalities resemble economies of scale, but they are not considered such because they are a function of the number of users of a good or service in an industry, not of the production efficiency within a business. _____ are only considered examples of network externalities if they are driven by demand side economies.

Formally, a production function ⬚> is defined to have:

- constant returns to scale if (for any constant a greater than or equal to 0) ⬚>
- increasing returns to scale if (for any constant a greater than 1) ⬚>
- decreasing returns to scale if (for any constant a greater than 1) ⬚>

where K and L are factors of production, capital and labour, respectively.

Chapter 6. Variability and Its Impact on Process Performance: Waiting Time Problems

As an example, the Cobb-Douglas functional form has constant returns to scale when the sum of the exponents adds up to one.

a. A4e
b. A Stake in the Outcome
c. Economies of scale external to the firm
d. AAAI

18. _____ is a service policy where by the requests of customers or clients are attended to in the order that they arrived, without other biases or preferences. The policy can be employed when processing sales orders, in determining restaurant seating, or on a taxi stand, for example.

Festival seating (also known as general seating and stadium seating) is seating done on a FCFS basis.

a. 28-hour day
b. 1990 Clean Air Act
c. 33 Strategies of War
d. First-come, first-served

19. The _____ model is a mathematical model in operations management and applied economics used to determine optimal inventory levels. It is (typically) characterized by fixed prices and uncertain demand. If the inventory level is q, each unit of demand above q is lost.

The standard _____ profit function is:

$$\boxed{}>$$

where D is a random variable representing demand, each unit is sold for price p and purchased for price c, and E is the expectation operator. The solution to the optimal stocking quantity of the _____ is:

$$\boxed{}>$$

where F^{-1} denotes the inverse cumulative distribution function of D.

a. 1990 Clean Air Act
b. Multiscale decision making
c. 28-hour day
d. Newsvendor

Chapter 7. The Impact of Variability on Process Performance: Throughput Losses

1. In queueing theory, _____ is the proportion of the system's resources which is used by the traffic which arrives at it. It should be strictly less than one for the system to function well. It is usually represented by the symbol ρ.

    a. A Stake in the Outcome
    b. A4e
    c. AAAI
    d. Utilization

2. In statistics, decision theory and economics, a _____ is a function that maps an event (technically an element of a sample space) onto a real number representing the economic cost or regret associated with the event.

    Less technically, in statistics a _____ represents the loss (cost in money or loss in utility in some other sense) associated with an estimate being 'wrong' (different from either a desired or a true value) as a function of a measure of the degree of wrongness (generally the difference between the estimated value and the true or desired value.)

    Both Frequentist and Bayesian statistical theory involve calculating statistics in such a way as to minimize the expected loss observed from being wrong given a set of assumptions about the data and one's _____.

    a. 1990 Clean Air Act
    b. 33 Strategies of War
    c. 28-hour day
    d. Loss Function

3. _____ is a way of expressing knowledge or belief that an event will occur or has occurred. In mathematics the concept has been given an exact meaning in _____ theory, that is used extensively in such areas of study as mathematics, statistics, finance, gambling, science, and philosophy to draw conclusions about the likelihood of potential events and the underlying mechanics of complex systems.

    The word _____ does not have a consistent direct definition.

    a. Statistics
    b. Time series analysis
    c. Standard deviation
    d. Probability

4. The _____ model is a mathematical model in operations management and applied economics used to determine optimal inventory levels. It is (typically) characterized by fixed prices and uncertain demand. If the inventory level is q, each unit of demand above q is lost.

    The standard _____ profit function is:

Chapter 7. The Impact of Variability on Process Performance: Throughput Losses

where D is a random variable representing demand, each unit is sold for price p and purchased for price c, and E is the expectation operator. The solution to the optimal stocking quantity of the _____ is:

where F^{-1} denotes the inverse cumulative distribution function of D.

a. Multiscale decision making
b. Newsvendor
c. 28-hour day
d. 1990 Clean Air Act

5. In economics, business, retail, and accounting, a _____ is the value of money that has been used up to produce something, and hence is not available for use anymore. In economics, a _____ is an alternative that is given up as a result of a decision. In business, the _____ may be one of acquisition, in which case the amount of money expended to acquire it is counted as _____.
    a. Cost allocation
    b. Fixed costs
    c. Cost
    d. Cost overrun

6. In decision theory and estimation theory, the _____ of an estimator, $\hat{\theta}$, of an unknown parameter of the distribution, θ, is the expected value of the loss function

$$R(\theta, \hat{\theta}) = \mathbb{E}_\theta L(\theta, \hat{\theta}) = \int L(\theta, \hat{\theta})\, dP_\theta.$$

where dP_θ is a probability measure parametrized by θ.

- For a scalar parameter θ and a quadratic loss function,

$$L(\theta, \hat{\theta}) = (\theta - \hat{\theta})^2$$

the _____ function becomes the mean squared error of the estimate,

$$R(\theta, \hat{\theta}) = E_\theta (\theta - \hat{\theta})^2$$

- In density estimation, the unknown parameter is probability density itself. The loss function is typically chosen to be a norm in an appropriate function space. For example, for L^2 norm,

$$L(f, \hat{f}) = \|f - \hat{f}\|_2^2$$

the _____ function becomes the mean integrated squared error

$$R(f, \hat{f}) = E\|f - \hat{f}\|^2$$

a. Linear model
b. Financial modeling
c. Risk aversion
d. Risk

Chapter 8. Quality Management, Statistical Process Control, and Six-Sigma Capability

1. _____ can be considered to have three main components: quality control, quality assurance and quality improvement. _____ is focused not only on product quality, but also the means to achieve it. _____ therefore uses quality assurance and control of processes as well as products to achieve more consistent quality.

   a. 1990 Clean Air Act
   b. 28-hour day
   c. Total quality management
   d. Quality management

2. _____ is one of the managerial functions like planning, organizing, staffing and directing. It is an important function because it helps to check the errors and to take the corrective action so that deviation from standards are minimized and stated goals of the organization are achieved in desired manner. According to modern concepts, _____ is a foreseeing action whereas earlier concept of _____ was used only when errors were detected. _____ in management means setting standards, measuring actual performance and taking corrective action.

   a. Decision tree pruning
   b. Turnover
   c. Schedule of reinforcement
   d. Control

3. _____ is an advertisement in which a particular product specifically mentions a competitor by name for the express purpose of showing why the competitor is inferior to the product naming it.

   This should not be confused with parody advertisements, where a fictional product is being advertised for the purpose of poking fun at the particular advertisement, nor should it be confused with the use of a coined brand name for the purpose of comparing the product without actually naming an actual competitor. ('Wikipedia tastes better and is less filling than the Encyclopedia Galactica.')

   In the 1980s, during what has been referred to as the cola wars, soft-drink manufacturer Pepsi ran a series of advertisements where people, caught on hidden camera, in a blind taste test, chose Pepsi over rival Coca-Cola.

   a. 1990 Clean Air Act
   b. 28-hour day
   c. 33 Strategies of War
   d. Comparative advertising

4. A _____ is a computer program typically used to provide some form of artificial intelligence, which consists primarily of a set of rules about behavior. These rules, termed productions, are a basic representation found useful in AI planning, expert systems and action selection. A _____ provides the mechanism necessary to execute productions in order to achieve some goal for the system.

Chapter 8. Quality Management, Statistical Process Control, and Six-Sigma Capability

a. 1990 Clean Air Act
b. 28-hour day
c. 33 Strategies of War
d. Production System

5. _____ is an effective method of monitoring a process through the use of control charts. Control charts enable the use of objective criteria for distinguishing background variation from events of significance based on statistical techniques. Much of its power lies in the ability to monitor both process center and its variation about that center.

a. Process capability
b. Quality control
c. Single Minute Exchange of Die
d. Statistical process control

6. The _____ in statistical process control is a tool used to determine whether a manufacturing or business process is in a state of statistical control or not.

If the chart indicates that the process is currently under control then it can be used with confidence to predict the future performance of the process. If the chart indicates that the process being monitored is not in control, the pattern it reveals can help determine the source of variation to be eliminated to bring the process back into control.

a. Control chart
b. Failure rate
c. Time series analysis
d. Simple moving average

7. An _____ is a specific member of a family of control charts. A control chart is a tool used in quality control, specifically SPC or statistical process control, as originally developed by Walter A. Shewhart at Western Electric in 1924 to improve the quality of telephones.

A control chart is a plot of measurements of a product on two special scales, usually located above and below each other and running horizontally. _____s consist of two charts, both with the same horizontal axis denoting the sample number.

a. 28-hour day
b. 1990 Clean Air Act
c. 33 Strategies of War
d. X-bar/R chart

Chapter 8. Quality Management, Statistical Process Control, and Six-Sigma Capability

8. The _____ is a measurable property of a process to the specification, expressed as a _____ index (e.g., C_{pk} or C_{pm}) or as a process performance index (e.g., P_{pk} or P_{pm}.) The output of this measurement is usually illustrated by a histogram and calculations that predict how many parts will be produced out of specification.

_____ is also defined as the capability of a process to meet its purpose as managed by an organization's management and process definition structures ISO 15504.

a. Quality control
b. Single Minute Exchange of Die
c. Statistical process control
d. Process capability

9. Engineering _____ is the permissible limit of variation in

1. a physical dimension,
2. a measured value or physical property of a material, manufactured object, system, or service,
3. other measured values (such as temperature, humidity, etc.)
4. in engineering and safety, a physical distance or space (_____), as in a truck (lorry), train or boat under a bridge as well as a train in a tunnel

Dimensions, properties, or conditions may vary within certain practical limits without significantly affecting functioning of equipment or a process. _____s are specified to allow reasonable leeway for imperfections and inherent variability without compromising performance.

The _____ may be specified as a factor or percentage of the nominal value, a maximum deviation from a nominal value, an explicit range of allowed values, be specified by a note or published standard with this information, or be implied by the numeric accuracy of the nominal value. _____ can be symmetrical, as in 40±0.1, or asymmetrical, such as 40+0.2/−0.1.

a. Tolerance
b. Root cause analysis
c. Quality assurance
d. Zero defects

10. In process improvement efforts, the _____ or process capability ratio is a statistical measure of process capability: The ability of a process to produce output within engineering tolerances and specification limits. The concept of process capability only holds meaning for processes that are in a state of statistical control.

If the upper and lower specifications of the process are USL and LSL, the target process mean is T, the estimated mean of the process is $\hat{\mu}$ and the estimated variability of the process (expressed as a standard deviation) is $\hat{\sigma}$, then commonly-accepted process capability indices include:

Chapter 8. Quality Management, Statistical Process Control, and Six-Sigma Capability

$\hat{\sigma}$ is estimated using the sample standard deviation.

a. Process capability ratio
b. 1990 Clean Air Act
c. Process capability index
d. Constant dollars

11. _____ are horizontal lines drawn on an statistical process control chart, usually at a distance of >±3 standard deviations of the plotted statistic from the statistic's mean.

For normally distributed statistics, the area bracketed by the _____ will on average contain 99.73% of all the plot points on the chart, as long as the process is and remains in statistical control.

_____ should not be confused with tolerance limits, which are completely independent of the distribution of the plotted sample statistic.

a. 1990 Clean Air Act
b. T-statistic
c. Skewness risk
d. Control limits

12. The _____ states that, for many events, roughly 80% of the effects come from 20% of the causes. Business management thinker Joseph M. Juran suggested the principle and named it after Italian economist Vilfredo Pareto, who observed that 80% of the land in Italy was owned by 20% of the population. It is a common rule of thumb in business; e.g., '80% of your sales come from 20% of your clients.' Mathematically, where something is shared among a sufficiently large set of participants, there will always be a number k between 50 and 100 such that k% is taken by% of the participants.
a. Bylaw
b. Board of directors
c. Greenfield agreement
d. Pareto principle

13. _____ is used for the design, development, analysis, and optimization of technical processes and is mainly applied to chemical plants and chemical processes, but also to power stations, and similar technical facilities. Process flow diagram of a typical amine treating process used in industrial plants

Chapter 8. Quality Management, Statistical Process Control, and Six-Sigma Capability

_____ is a model-based representation of chemical, physical, biological, and other technical processes and unit operations in software. Basic prerequisites are a thorough knowledge of chemical and physical properties of pure components and mixtures, of reactions, and of mathematical models which, in combination, allow the calculation of a process in computers.

a. Process simulation
b. 1990 Clean Air Act
c. 28-hour day
d. 33 Strategies of War

14. _____ is the process of understanding, anticipating and influencing consumer behavior in order to maximize revenue or profits from a fixed, perishable resource This process was first discovered by Dr. Matt H. Keller. The challenge is to sell the right resources to the right customer at the right time for the right price.

a. Gap analysis
b. Business networking
c. Business model design
d. Yield management

15. In economics, business, retail, and accounting, a _____ is the value of money that has been used up to produce something, and hence is not available for use anymore. In economics, a _____ is an alternative that is given up as a result of a decision. In business, the _____ may be one of acquisition, in which case the amount of money expended to acquire it is counted as _____.

a. Cost allocation
b. Cost overrun
c. Cost
d. Fixed costs

16. In organizational development (OD), _____ is a series of actions taken by a Process Owner to identify, analyze and improve existing processes within an organization to meet new goals and objectives. These actions often follow a specific methodology or strategy to create successful results. A sampling of these are listed below.

a. Supervisory board
b. Letter of resignation
c. Product innovation
d. Process improvement

Chapter 9. Lean Operations and the Toyota Production System

1. A _____ is a computer program typically used to provide some form of artificial intelligence, which consists primarily of a set of rules about behavior. These rules, termed productions, are a basic representation found useful in AI planning, expert systems and action selection. A _____ provides the mechanism necessary to execute productions in order to achieve some goal for the system.
    a. 1990 Clean Air Act
    b. 28-hour day
    c. 33 Strategies of War
    d. Production System

2. _____ can be considered to have three main components: quality control, quality assurance and quality improvement. _____ is focused not only on product quality, but also the means to achieve it. _____ therefore uses quality assurance and control of processes as well as products to achieve more consistent quality.
    a. 28-hour day
    b. Total quality management
    c. 1990 Clean Air Act
    d. Quality management

3. Autonomation describes a feature of machine design to effect the principle of _____ used in the Toyota Production System (TPS) and Lean manufacturing. It may be described as 'intelligent automation' or 'automation with a human touch.' This type of automation implements some supervisory functions rather than production functions. At Toyota this usually means that if an abnormal situation arises the machine stops and the worker will stop the production line.
    a. Jidoka
    b. Manufacturing resource planning
    c. Homeworkers
    d. MRP II

4. _____ is a Japanese philosophy that focuses on continuous improvement throughout all aspects of life. When applied to the workplace, _____ activities continually improve all functions of a business, from manufacturing to management and from the CEO to the assembly line workers. By improving standardized activities and processes, _____ aims to eliminate waste.
    a. Sensitivity analysis
    b. Cross-docking
    c. Psychological pricing
    d. Kaizen

5. _____ is a concept related to lean and just-in-time (JIT) production. The Japanese word _____ is a common term meaning 'signboard' or 'billboard'. According to Taiichi Ohno, the man credited with developing JIT, _____ is a means through which JIT is achieved.

Chapter 9. Lean Operations and the Toyota Production System

a. Succession planning
b. Trademark
c. Kanban
d. Risk management

6. _____ is a Japanese term that means 'fail-safing' or 'mistake-proofing'. A _____ is any mechanism in a Lean manufacturing process that helps an equipment operator avoid (yokeru) mistakes (poka.) Its purpose is to eliminate product defects by preventing, correcting, or drawing attention to human errors as they occur.
   a. 33 Strategies of War
   b. 28-hour day
   c. 1990 Clean Air Act
   d. Poka-yoke

7. A _____ is a volunteer group composed of workers (or even students), usually under the leadership of their supervisor (but they can elect a team leader), who are trained to identify, analyse and solve work-related problems and present their solutions to management in order to improve the performance of the organization, and motivate and enrich the work of employees. When matured, true _____s become self-managing, having gained the confidence of management.
   _____s are an alternative to the dehumanising concept of the Division of Labour, where workers or individuals are treated like robots.
   a. Connectionist expert systems
   b. Competency-based job descriptions
   c. Certified in Production and Inventory Management
   d. Quality circle

8. _____ can be defined as the maximum time per unit allowed to produce a product in order to meet demand. It is derived from the German word Taktzeit which translates to cycle time. _____ sets the pace for industrial manufacturing lines. In automobile manufacturing, for example, cars are assembled on a line, and are moved on to the next station after a certain time - the _____. Therefore, the time needed to complete work on each station has to be less than the _____ in order for the product to be completed within the alloted time.
   a. Six Sigma
   b. Theory of constraints
   c. Production line
   d. Takt time

9. '_____' is Step 7 of 'Philip Crosby's 14 Step Quality Improvement Process'. Although applicable to any type of enterprise, it has been primarily adopted within industry supply chains wherever large volumes of components are being purchased (common items such as nuts and bolts are good examples.)

Chapter 9. Lean Operations and the Toyota Production System

_____ was a quality control program originated by the Denver Division of the Martin Marietta Corporation (now Lockheed Martin) on the Titan Missile program, which carried the first astronauts into space in the late 1960s.

   a. Root cause analysis
   b. Zero defects
   c. 28-hour day
   d. 1990 Clean Air Act

10. _____ is one of the managerial functions like planning, organizing, staffing and directing. It is an important function because it helps to check the errors and to take the corrective action so that deviation from standards are minimized and stated goals of the organization are achieved in desired manner. According to modern concepts, _____ is a foreseeing action whereas earlier concept of _____ was used only when errors were detected. _____ in management means setting standards, measuring actual performance and taking corrective action.
   a. Decision tree pruning
   b. Control
   c. Schedule of reinforcement
   d. Turnover

11. _____ is an advertisement in which a particular product specifically mentions a competitor by name for the express purpose of showing why the competitor is inferior to the product naming it.

This should not be confused with parody advertisements, where a fictional product is being advertised for the purpose of poking fun at the particular advertisement, nor should it be confused with the use of a coined brand name for the purpose of comparing the product without actually naming an actual competitor. ('Wikipedia tastes better and is less filling than the Encyclopedia Galactica.')

In the 1980s, during what has been referred to as the cola wars, soft-drink manufacturer Pepsi ran a series of advertisements where people, caught on hidden camera, in a blind taste test, chose Pepsi over rival Coca-Cola.

   a. 1990 Clean Air Act
   b. 28-hour day
   c. 33 Strategies of War
   d. Comparative advertising

12. The _____ was a period in the late 18th and early 19th centuries when major changes in agriculture, manufacturing, mining, and transportation had a profound effect on the socioeconomic and cultural conditions in Britain. The changes subsequently spread throughout Europe, North America, and eventually the world. The onset of the _____ marked a major turning point in human society; almost every aspect of daily life was eventually influenced in some way.

Chapter 9. Lean Operations and the Toyota Production System

a. Abraham Harold Maslow
b. Adam Smith
c. Affiliation
d. Industrial revolution

13. In decision theory and estimation theory, the _____ of an estimator, $\hat{\theta}$, of an unknown parameter of the distribution, θ, is the expected value of the loss function

$$R(\theta, \hat{\theta}) = \mathbb{E}_\theta L(\theta, \hat{\theta}) = \int L(\theta, \hat{\theta}) \, dP_\theta.$$

where dP_θ is a probability measure parametrized by θ.

- For a scalar parameter θ and a quadratic loss function,

$$L(\theta, \hat{\theta}) = (\theta - \hat{\theta})^2$$

the _____ function becomes the mean squared error of the estimate,

$$R(\theta, \hat{\theta}) = E_\theta (\theta - \hat{\theta})^2$$

- In density estimation, the unknown parameter is probability density itself. The loss function is typically chosen to be a norm in an appropriate function space. For example, for L^2 norm,

$$L(f, \hat{f}) = \|f - \hat{f}\|_2^2$$

the _____ function becomes the mean integrated squared error

$$R(f, \hat{f}) = E\|f - \hat{f}\|^2$$

a. Linear model
b. Financial modeling
c. Risk aversion
d. Risk

Chapter 9. Lean Operations and the Toyota Production System

14. _____, widely known as F. W. Taylor, was an American mechanical engineer who sought to improve industrial efficiency. He is regarded as the father of scientific management, and was one of the first management consultants.

Taylor was one of the intellectual leaders of the Efficiency Movement and his ideas, broadly conceived, were highly influential in the Progressive Era.

a. Jonah Jacob Goldberg
b. Douglas N. Daft
c. Geoffrey Colvin
d. Frederick Winslow Taylor

15. _____ is an inventory strategy that strives to improve the return on investment of a business by reducing in-process inventory and its associated carrying costs. To meet _____ objectives, the process relies on signals between different points in the process. This means the process is often driven by a series of signals, or Kanban , which tell production when to make the next part. Kanban are usually 'tickets' but can be simple visual signals, such as the presence or absence of a part on a shelf. Implemented correctly, _____ can dramatically improve a manufacturing organization's return on investment, quality, and efficiency.

a. 1990 Clean Air Act
b. 33 Strategies of War
c. Just-in-time
d. 28-hour day

16. _____ is a company-wide computer software system used to manage and coordinate all the resources, information, and functions of a business from shared data stores.

An _____ system has a service-oriented architecture with modular hardware and software units and 'services' that communicate on a local area network. The modular design allows a business to add or reconfigure modules (perhaps from different vendors) while preserving data integrity in one shared database that may be centralized or distributed.

a. A Stake in the Outcome
b. AAAI
c. A4e
d. Enterprise resource planning

17. The metastability in flip-flops can be avoided by ensuring that the data and control inputs are held valid and constant for specified periods before and after the clock pulse, called the _____ and the hold time (t_h) respectively. These times are specified in the data sheet for the device, and are typically between a few nanoseconds and a few hundred picoseconds for modern devices.

Chapter 9. Lean Operations and the Toyota Production System

Unfortunately, it is not always possible to meet the setup and hold criteria, because the flip-flop may be connected to a real-time signal that could change at any time, outside the control of the designer.

a. Setup time
b. 28-hour day
c. 33 Strategies of War
d. 1990 Clean Air Act

18. In economics, _____ is the desire to own something and the ability to pay for it. The term _____ signifies the ability or the willingness to buy a particular commodity at a given point of time.
a. 33 Strategies of War
b. 1990 Clean Air Act
c. Demand
d. 28-hour day

19. _____ is an increasingly broadening term with which an organization, or other human system describes the combination of traditionally administrative personnel functions with acquisition and application of skills, knowledge and experience, Employee Relations and resource planning at various levels. The field draws upon concepts developed in Industrial/Organizational Psychology and System Theory. _____ has at least two related interpretations depending on context. The original usage derives from political economy and economics, where it was traditionally called labor, one of four factors of production although this perspective is changing as a function of new and ongoing research into more strategic approaches at national levels. This first usage is used more in terms of '_____ development', and can go beyond just organizations to the level of nations . The more traditional usage within corporations and businesses refers to the individuals within a firm or agency, and to the portion of the organization that deals with hiring, firing, training, and other personnel issues, typically referred to as `_____ management'.
a. Human resource management
b. Bradford Factor
c. Progressive discipline
d. Human resources

20. _____s are diagrams that show the causes of a certain event. A common use of the _____ is in product design, to identify potential factors causing an overall effect.

_____s were proposed by Kaoru Ishikawa in the 1960s, who pioneered quality management processes in the Kawasaki shipyards, and in the process became one of the founding fathers of modern management.

Chapter 9. Lean Operations and the Toyota Production System

a. A Stake in the Outcome
b. Ishikawa diagram
c. AAAI
d. A4e

Chapter 10. Betting on Uncertain Demand: The Newsvendor Model

1. The _____ model is a mathematical model in operations management and applied economics used to determine optimal inventory levels. It is (typically) characterized by fixed prices and uncertain demand. If the inventory level is q, each unit of demand above q is lost.

The standard _____ profit function is:

where D is a random variable representing demand, each unit is sold for price p and purchased for price c, and E is the expectation operator. The solution to the optimal stocking quantity of the _____ is:

where F^{-1} denotes the inverse cumulative distribution function of D.

   a. 28-hour day
   b. Multiscale decision making
   c. Newsvendor
   d. 1990 Clean Air Act

2. In economics, business, retail, and accounting, a _____ is the value of money that has been used up to produce something, and hence is not available for use anymore. In economics, a _____ is an alternative that is given up as a result of a decision. In business, the _____ may be one of acquisition, in which case the amount of money expended to acquire it is counted as _____.
   a. Cost overrun
   b. Cost allocation
   c. Fixed costs
   d. Cost

3. In economics, _____ is the desire to own something and the ability to pay for it. The term _____ signifies the ability or the willingness to buy a particular commodity at a given point of time.
   a. 33 Strategies of War
   b. Demand
   c. 1990 Clean Air Act
   d. 28-hour day

4. In economics, _____ are business expenses that are not dependent on the activities of the business They tend to be time-related, such as salaries or rents being paid per month. This is in contrast to variable costs, which are volume-related (and are paid per quantity.)

Chapter 10. Betting on Uncertain Demand: The Newsvendor Model

In management accounting, _____ are defined as expenses that do not change in proportion to the activity of a business, within the relevant period or scale of production.

a. Fixed costs
b. Transaction cost
c. Cost of quality
d. Cost allocation

5. _____ is the process of estimation in unknown situations. Prediction is a similar, but more general term. Both can refer to estimation of time series, cross-sectional or longitudinal data.
a. 33 Strategies of War
b. 1990 Clean Air Act
c. Forecasting
d. 28-hour day

6. In the fields of science, engineering, industry and statistics, _____ is the degree of closeness of a measured or calculated quantity to its actual (true) value. _____ is closely related to precision, also called reproducibility or repeatability, the degree to which further measurements or calculations show the same or similar results. _____ indicates proximity to the true value, precision to the repeatability or reproducibility of the measurement

The results of calculations or a measurement can be accurate but not precise, precise but not accurate, neither, or both.

a. AAAI
b. A Stake in the Outcome
c. Accuracy
d. A4e

7. _____ is the activity of estimating the quantity of a product or service that consumers will purchase. _____ involves techniques including both informal methods, such as educated guesses, and quantitative methods, such as the use of historical sales data or current data from test markets. _____ may be used in making pricing decisions, in assessing future capacity requirements, or in making decisions on whether to enter a new market.
a. Demand Forecasting
b. 28-hour day
c. Profitability index
d. 1990 Clean Air Act

Chapter 10. Betting on Uncertain Demand: The Newsvendor Model

8. In probability theory, a probability distribution is called _____ if its cumulative distribution function is _____. This is equivalent to saying that for random variables X with the distribution in question, Pr[X = a] = 0 for all real numbers a, i.e.: the probability that X attains the value a is zero, for any number a. If the distribution of X is _____ then X is called a _____ random variable.

   a. Decision tree pruning
   b. Continuous
   c. Connectionist expert systems
   d. Pay Band

9. In probability theory and statistics, a _____ identifies either the probability of each value of an unidentified random variable (when the variable is discrete), or the probability of the value falling within a particular interval (when the variable is continuous.) The _____ describes the range of possible values that a random variable can attain and the probability that the value of the random variable is within any (measurable) subset of that range. The Normal distribution, often called the 'bell curve'

   When the random variable takes values in the set of real numbers, the _____ is completely described by the cumulative distribution function, whose value at each real x is the probability that the random variable is smaller than or equal to x.

   a. Median
   b. Probability distribution
   c. Frequency distribution
   d. Statistically significant

10. _____ is one of the four elements of marketing mix. An organization or set of organizations (go-betweens) involved in the process of making a product or service available for use or consumption by a consumer or business user.

    The other three parts of the marketing mix are product, pricing, and promotion.

    a. Missing completely at random
    b. Job creation programs
    c. Matching theory
    d. Distribution

11. A _____ is a list of the general tasks and responsibilities of a position. Typically, it also includes to whom the position reports, specifications such as the qualifications needed by the person in the job, salary range for the position, etc. A _____ is usually developed by conducting a job analysis, which includes examining the tasks and sequences of tasks necessary to perform the job.

a. Job description
b. Recruitment Process Insourcing
c. Recruitment advertising
d. Recruitment

12. In probability theory and statistics, the _____ or Gaussian distribution is a continuous probability distribution that describes data that clusters around a mean or average. The graph of the associated probability density function is bell-shaped, with a peak at the mean, and is known as the Gaussian function or bell curve.

The _____ can be used to describe, at least approximately, any variable that tends to cluster around the mean.

a. Normal Distribution
b. Histogram
c. Generalized normal distribution
d. Heteroskedastic

13. In probability and statistics the _____ is a discrete probability distribution. It arises as the probability distribution of the number of failures in a sequence of Bernoulli trials needed to get a specified (non-random) number of successes. If one throws a die repeatedly until the third time a '1' appears, then the probability distribution of the number of non-'1's that appear before the third '1' is a _____.
a. 28-hour day
b. 33 Strategies of War
c. 1990 Clean Air Act
d. Negative binomial distribution

14. In probability theory and statistics, the _____ is the discrete probability distribution of the number of successes in a sequence of n independent yes/no experiments, each of which yields success with probability p. Such a success/failure experiment is also called a Bernoulli experiment or Bernoulli trial. In fact, when n = 1, the _____ is a Bernoulli distribution.
a. Statistics
b. Probability
c. Discrete probability distributions
d. Binomial distribution

Chapter 10. Betting on Uncertain Demand: The Newsvendor Model

15. _____ or economic opportunity loss is the value of the next best alternative forgone as the result of making a decision. _____ analysis is an important part of a company's decision-making processes but is not treated as an actual cost in any financial statement. The next best thing that a person can engage in is referred to as the _____ of doing the best thing and ignoring the next best thing to be done.

   a. A4e
   b. AAAI
   c. Opportunity cost
   d. A Stake in the Outcome

16. In statistics, decision theory and economics, a _____ is a function that maps an event (technically an element of a sample space) onto a real number representing the economic cost or regret associated with the event.

   Less technically, in statistics a _____ represents the loss (cost in money or loss in utility in some other sense) associated with an estimate being 'wrong' (different from either a desired or a true value) as a function of a measure of the degree of wrongness (generally the difference between the estimated value and the true or desired value.)

   Both Frequentist and Bayesian statistical theory involve calculating statistics in such a way as to minimize the expected loss observed from being wrong given a set of assumptions about the data and one's _____.

   a. Loss Function
   b. 33 Strategies of War
   c. 1990 Clean Air Act
   d. 28-hour day

17. In decision theory and estimation theory, the _____ of an estimator, $\hat{\theta}$, of an unknown parameter of the distribution, θ, is the expected value of the loss function

$$R(\theta, \hat{\theta}) = \mathbb{E}_\theta L(\theta, \hat{\theta}) = \int L(\theta, \hat{\theta})\, dP_\theta.$$

Chapter 10. Betting on Uncertain Demand: The Newsvendor Model

where dP_θ is a probability measure parametrized by θ.

- For a scalar parameter θ and a quadratic loss function,

$$L(\theta, \hat{\theta}) = (\theta - \hat{\theta})^2$$

the _____ function becomes the mean squared error of the estimate,

$$R(\theta, \hat{\theta}) = E_\theta(\theta - \hat{\theta})^2$$

- In density estimation, the unknown parameter is probability density itself. The loss function is typically chosen to be a norm in an appropriate function space. For example, for L^2 norm,

$$L(f, \hat{f}) = \|f - \hat{f}\|_2^2$$

the _____ function becomes the mean integrated squared error

$$R(f, \hat{f}) = E\|f - \hat{f}\|^2$$

a. Risk
b. Financial modeling
c. Linear model
d. Risk aversion

18. _____ is a way of expressing knowledge or belief that an event will occur or has occurred. In mathematics the concept has been given an exact meaning in _____ theory, that is used extensively in such areas of study as mathematics, statistics, finance, gambling, science, and philosophy to draw conclusions about the likelihood of potential events and the underlying mechanics of complex systems.

The word _____ does not have a consistent direct definition.

a. Probability
b. Standard deviation
c. Time series analysis
d. Statistics

Chapter 11. Assemble-to-Order, Make-to-Order, and Quick Response with Reactive Capacity

1. The _____ model is a mathematical model in operations management and applied economics used to determine optimal inventory levels. It is (typically) characterized by fixed prices and uncertain demand. If the inventory level is q, each unit of demand above q is lost.

The standard _____ profit function is:

$$\,$$

where D is a random variable representing demand, each unit is sold for price p and purchased for price c, and E is the expectation operator. The solution to the optimal stocking quantity of the _____ is:

$$\,$$

where F^{-1} denotes the inverse cumulative distribution function of D.

   a. 28-hour day
   b. Multiscale decision making
   c. 1990 Clean Air Act
   d. Newsvendor

2. _____ is a broad label that refers to any individuals or households that use goods and services generated within the economy. The concept of a _____ is used in different contexts, so that the usage and significance of the term may vary.

Typically when business people and economists talk of _____s they are talking about person as _____, an aggregated commodity item with little individuality other than that expressed in the buy/not-buy decision.

   a. 33 Strategies of War
   b. 1990 Clean Air Act
   c. 28-hour day
   d. Consumer

3. In economics, business, retail, and accounting, a _____ is the value of money that has been used up to produce something, and hence is not available for use anymore. In economics, a _____ is an alternative that is given up as a result of a decision. In business, the _____ may be one of acquisition, in which case the amount of money expended to acquire it is counted as _____.

Chapter 11. Assemble-to-Order, Make-to-Order, and Quick Response with Reactive Capacity

a. Fixed costs
b. Cost overrun
c. Cost allocation
d. Cost

4. _____ is a joint trade and industry body working towards making the grocery sector as a whole more responsive to consumer demand and promote the removal of unnecessary costs from the supply chain.

The _____ movement beginning in the mid-nineties was characterized by the emergence of new principles of collaborative management along the supply chain. It was understood that companies can serve consumers better, faster and at less cost by working together with trading partners.

a. Entertainment Management
b. Event management
c. Exception management
d. Efficient Consumer Response

5. In statistics, decision theory and economics, a _____ is a function that maps an event (technically an element of a sample space) onto a real number representing the economic cost or regret associated with the event.

Less technically, in statistics a _____ represents the loss (cost in money or loss in utility in some other sense) associated with an estimate being 'wrong' (different from either a desired or a true value) as a function of a measure of the degree of wrongness (generally the difference between the estimated value and the true or desired value.)

Both Frequentist and Bayesian statistical theory involve calculating statistics in such a way as to minimize the expected loss observed from being wrong given a set of assumptions about the data and one's _____.

a. 28-hour day
b. 33 Strategies of War
c. 1990 Clean Air Act
d. Loss Function

6. In probability theory and statistics, the _____ is a normalized measure of dispersion of a probability distribution. It is defined as the ratio of the standard deviation σ to the mean μ:

$$c_v = \frac{\sigma}{\mu}$$

This is only defined for non-zero mean, and is most useful for variables that are always positive. It is also known as unitized risk.

a. Failure rate
b. Frequency distribution
c. Control chart
d. Coefficient of variation

Chapter 12. Service Levels and Lead Times in Supply Chains: The Order-up-to Inventory Model

1. _____ are goods that have completed the manufacturing process but have not yet been sold or distributed to the end user.

Manufacturing has three classes of inventory:

1. Raw material
2. Work in process
3. _____

A good purchased as a 'raw material' goes into the manufacture of a product. A good only partially completed during the manufacturing process is called 'work in process'. When the good is completed as to manufacturing but not yet sold or distributed to the end-user is called a 'finished good'.

a. Finished goods
b. Reorder point
c. 1990 Clean Air Act
d. 28-hour day

2. In decision theory and estimation theory, the _____ of an estimator, $\hat{\theta}$, of an unknown parameter of the distribution, θ, is the expected value of the loss function

$$R(\theta, \hat{\theta}) = \mathbb{E}_\theta L(\theta, \hat{\theta}) = \int L(\theta, \hat{\theta}) \, dP_\theta.$$

where dP_θ is a probability measure parametrized by θ.

- For a scalar parameter θ and a quadratic loss function,

$$L(\theta, \hat{\theta}) = (\theta - \hat{\theta})^2$$

the _____ function becomes the mean squared error of the estimate,

$$R(\theta, \hat{\theta}) = E_\theta (\theta - \hat{\theta})^2$$

- In density estimation, the unknown parameter is probability density itself. The loss function is typically chosen to be a norm in an appropriate function space. For example, for L^2 norm,

$$L(f, \hat{f}) = \|f - \hat{f}\|_2^2$$

the _____ function becomes the mean integrated squared error

$$R(f, \hat{f}) = E\|f - \hat{f}\|^2$$

a. Linear model
b. Risk aversion
c. Financial modeling
d. Risk

3. The _____ is an observed phenomenon in forecast-driven distribution channels. The concept has its roots in J Forrester's Industrial Dynamics (1961) and thus it is also known as the Forrester Effect. Since the oscillating demand magnification upstream a supply chain reminds someone of a cracking whip it became famous as the _____.
a. Bullwhip effect
b. 33 Strategies of War
c. 1990 Clean Air Act
d. 28-hour day

4. In economics, business, retail, and accounting, a _____ is the value of money that has been used up to produce something, and hence is not available for use anymore. In economics, a _____ is an alternative that is given up as a result of a decision. In business, the _____ may be one of acquisition, in which case the amount of money expended to acquire it is counted as _____.

Chapter 12. Service Levels and Lead Times in Supply Chains: The Order-up-to Inventory Model

a. Cost
b. Cost allocation
c. Cost overrun
d. Fixed costs

5. In economics, _____ is the desire to own something and the ability to pay for it. The term _____ signifies the ability or the willingness to buy a particular commodity at a given point of time.

a. 28-hour day
b. 1990 Clean Air Act
c. 33 Strategies of War
d. Demand

6. A _____ is the period of time between the initiation of any process of production and the completion of that process. Thus the _____ for ordering a new car from a manufacturer may be anywhere from 2 weeks to 6 months. In industry, _____ reduction is an important part of lean manufacturing.

a. 33 Strategies of War
b. 1990 Clean Air Act
c. 28-hour day
d. Lead time

7. _____ is a concept related to lean and just-in-time (JIT) production. The Japanese word _____ is a common term meaning 'signboard' or 'billboard'. According to Taiichi Ohno, the man credited with developing JIT, _____ is a means through which JIT is achieved.

a. Kanban
b. Trademark
c. Succession planning
d. Risk management

8. _____ is one of the managerial functions like planning, organizing, staffing and directing. It is an important function because it helps to check the errors and to take the corrective action so that deviation from standards are minimized and stated goals of the organization are achieved in desired manner. According to modern concepts, _____ is a foreseeing action whereas earlier concept of _____ was used only when errors were detected. _____ in management means setting standards, measuring actual performance and taking corrective action.

Chapter 12. Service Levels and Lead Times in Supply Chains: The Order-up-to Inventory Model

a. Decision tree pruning
b. Schedule of reinforcement
c. Turnover
d. Control

9. A _____ is typically described as a deliberate plan of action to guide decisions and achieve rational outcome(s.) However, the term may also be used to denote what is actually done, even though it is unplanned.

The term may apply to government, private sector organizations and groups, and individuals.

a. 33 Strategies of War
b. 1990 Clean Air Act
c. 28-hour day
d. Policy

10. _____ is an advertisement in which a particular product specifically mentions a competitor by name for the express purpose of showing why the competitor is inferior to the product naming it.

This should not be confused with parody advertisements, where a fictional product is being advertised for the purpose of poking fun at the particular advertisement, nor should it be confused with the use of a coined brand name for the purpose of comparing the product without actually naming an actual competitor. ('Wikipedia tastes better and is less filling than the Encyclopedia Galactica.')

In the 1980s, during what has been referred to as the cola wars, soft-drink manufacturer Pepsi ran a series of advertisements where people, caught on hidden camera, in a blind taste test, chose Pepsi over rival Coca-Cola.

a. 28-hour day
b. 1990 Clean Air Act
c. 33 Strategies of War
d. Comparative advertising

11. _____ is one of the four elements of marketing mix. An organization or set of organizations (go-betweens) involved in the process of making a product or service available for use or consumption by a consumer or business user.

The other three parts of the marketing mix are product, pricing, and promotion.

Chapter 12. Service Levels and Lead Times in Supply Chains: The Order-up-to Inventory Model

a. Matching theory
b. Missing completely at random
c. Job creation programs
d. Distribution

12. In probability theory and statistics, _____ is a measure of the variability or dispersion of a population, a data set, or a probability distribution. A low _____ indicates that the data points tend to be very close to the same value (the mean), while high _____ indicates that the data are 'spread out' over a large range of values.

For example, the average height for adult men in the United States is about 70 inches (178 cm), with a _____ of around 3 in (8 cm.)

a. Normal distribution
b. Frequency distribution
c. Failure rate
d. Standard deviation

13. _____ is a way of expressing knowledge or belief that an event will occur or has occurred. In mathematics the concept has been given an exact meaning in _____ theory, that is used extensively in such areas of study as mathematics, statistics, finance, gambling, science, and philosophy to draw conclusions about the likelihood of potential events and the underlying mechanics of complex systems.

The word _____ does not have a consistent direct definition.

a. Time series analysis
b. Statistics
c. Standard deviation
d. Probability

14. In business management, _____ is money spent to keep and maintain a stock of goods in storage.

The most obvious _____s include rent for the required space; equipment, materials, and labor to operate the space; insurance; security; interest on money invested in the inventory and space, and other direct expenses. Some stored goods become obsolete before they are sold, reducing their contribution to revenue while having no effect on their _____.

Chapter 12. Service Levels and Lead Times in Supply Chains: The Order-up-to Inventory Model

a. Choquet integral
b. Market niche
c. Private placement
d. Holding cost

15. _____ measures the performance of a system. Certain goals are defined and the _____ gives the percentage to which they should be achieved.

Examples

- Percentage of calls answered in a call center.
- Percentage of customers waiting less than a given fixed time.
- Percentage of customers that do not experience a stock out.

_____ is used in supply chain management and in inventory management to measure the performance of inventory systems.

Under stochastic conditions it is unavoidable that in some periods the inventory on hand is not sufficient to deliver the complete demand and, as a consequence, that part of the demand is filled only after an inventory-related waiting time.

a. 28-hour day
b. 1990 Clean Air Act
c. 33 Strategies of War
d. Service level

16. _____ Management is the succession of strategies used by management as a product goes through its _____. The conditions in which a product is sold changes over time and must be managed as it moves through its succession of stages.

The _____ goes through many phases, involves many professional disciplines, and requires many skills, tools and processes.

a. Golden handshake
b. Job hunting
c. Product life cycle
d. Strategic Alliance

Chapter 12. Service Levels and Lead Times in Supply Chains: The Order-up-to Inventory Model

17. _____ is the level of inventory that minimizes the total inventory holding costs and ordering costs. The framework used to determine this order quantity is also known as Wilson _____ Model. The model was developed by F. W. Harris in 1913.
   a. Anti-leadership
   b. Event management
   c. Effective executive
   d. Economic order quantity

18. In a human resources context, _____ or labor _____ is the rate at which an employer gains and loses employees. Simple ways to describe it are 'how long employees tend to stay' or 'the rate of traffic through the revolving door.' _____ is measured for individual companies and for their industry as a whole. If an employer is said to have a high _____ relative to its competitors, it means that employees of that company have a shorter average tenure than those of other companies in the same industry.
   a. Continuous
   b. Career portfolios
   c. Ten year occupational employment projection
   d. Turnover

19. The _____ is an equation that equals the cost of goods sold divided by the average inventory. Average inventory equals beginning inventory plus ending inventory divided by 2.

The formula for _____:

The formula for average inventory:

A low turnover rate may point to overstocking, obsolescence, or deficiencies in the product line or marketing effort.

   a. A Stake in the Outcome
   b. Asset turnover
   c. A4e
   d. Inventory turnover

Chapter 12. Service Levels and Lead Times in Supply Chains: The Order-up-to Inventory Model

20. _____ is a practice in logistics of unloading materials from an incoming semi-trailer truck or rail car and loading these materials directly into outbound trucks, trailers with little or no storage in between. This may be done to change type of conveyance, to sort material intended for different destinations or similar destination.

Cross-Dock operations were first pioneered in the US trucking industry in the 1930's, and have been in continuous use in LTL (less than truckload) operations ever since.

    a. Product life cycle
    b. Small business
    c. Corporate recovery
    d. Cross-docking

Chapter 13. Risk-Pooling Strategies to Reduce and Hedge Uncertainty

1. In decision theory and estimation theory, the _____ of an estimator, $\hat{\theta}$, of an unknown parameter of the distribution, θ, is the expected value of the loss function

$$R(\theta, \hat{\theta}) = \mathbb{E}_\theta L(\theta, \hat{\theta}) = \int L(\theta, \hat{\theta})\, dP_\theta.$$

where dP_θ is a probability measure parametrized by θ.

- For a scalar parameter θ and a quadratic loss function,

$$L(\theta, \hat{\theta}) = (\theta - \hat{\theta})^2$$

the _____ function becomes the mean squared error of the estimate,

$$R(\theta, \hat{\theta}) = E_\theta(\theta - \hat{\theta})^2$$

- In density estimation, the unknown parameter is probability density itself. The loss function is typically chosen to be a norm in an appropriate function space. For example, for L^2 norm,

$$L(f, \hat{f}) = \|f - \hat{f}\|_2^2$$

the _____ function becomes the mean integrated squared error

$$R(f, \hat{f}) = E\|f - \hat{f}\|^2$$

a. Linear model
b. Risk
c. Financial modeling
d. Risk aversion

2. In economics, business, retail, and accounting, a _____ is the value of money that has been used up to produce something, and hence is not available for use anymore. In economics, a _____ is an alternative that is given up as a result of a decision. In business, the _____ may be one of acquisition, in which case the amount of money expended to acquire it is counted as _____.

a. Cost allocation
b. Fixed costs
c. Cost overrun
d. Cost

3. _____ is one of the four elements of marketing mix. An organization or set of organizations (go-betweens) involved in the process of making a product or service available for use or consumption by a consumer or business user.

The other three parts of the marketing mix are product, pricing, and promotion.

a. Missing completely at random
b. Matching theory
c. Job creation programs
d. Distribution

4. A _____ for a set of products is a warehouse or other specialized building, often with refrigeration or air conditioning, which is stocked with products (goods) to be re-distributed to retailers, wholesalers or directly to consumers. A _____ is a principle part, the 'order processing' element, of the entire 'order fulfillment' process. _____s are usually thought of as being 'demand driven'.
a. Third-party logistics
b. 28-hour day
c. 1990 Clean Air Act
d. Distribution center

5. _____, commonly known as e-commerce, consists of the buying and selling of products or services over electronic systems such as the Internet and other computer networks. The amount of trade conducted electronically has grown extraordinarily with widespread Internet usage. The use of commerce is conducted in this way, spurring and drawing on innovations in electronic funds transfer, supply chain management, Internet marketing, online transaction processing, electronic data interchange (EDI), inventory management systems, and automated data collection systems.
a. Online shopping
b. A4e
c. Electronic Commerce
d. A Stake in the Outcome

6. _____ is a supply chain management technique in which the retailer does not keep goods in stock, but instead transfers customer orders and shipment details to either the manufacturer or a wholesaler, who then ships the goods directly to the customer. As in all retail businesses, the retailers make their profit on the difference between the wholesale and retail price.

Chapter 13. Risk-Pooling Strategies to Reduce and Hedge Uncertainty

Some _____ retailers may keep 'show' items on display in stores, so that customers can inspect an item similar to those that they can purchase.

a. Drop shipping
b. Freight forwarder
c. Supply chain
d. Packaging

7. _____ is a relatively new paradigm that emerged from 'barrier-free' or 'accessible design' and 'assistive technology.' _____ strives to be a broad-spectrum solution that produces buildings, products and environments that are usable and effective for everyone, not just people with disabilities. Moreover, it recognizes the importance of how things look. For example, while built up handles are a way to make utensils more usable for people with gripping limitations, some companies introduced larger, easy to grip and attractive handles as feature of mass produced utensils.

a. AAAI
b. Universal design
c. A Stake in the Outcome
d. A4e

8. In probability theory and statistics, the _____ is a normalized measure of dispersion of a probability distribution. It is defined as the ratio of the standard deviation σ to the mean μ:

$$c_v = \frac{\sigma}{\mu}$$

This is only defined for non-zero mean, and is most useful for variables that are always positive. It is also known as unitized risk.

a. Failure rate
b. Control chart
c. Coefficient of variation
d. Frequency distribution

9. In statistics, _____ indicates the strength and direction of a linear relationship between two random variables. That is in contrast with the usage of the term in colloquial speech, which denotes any relationship, not necessarily linear. In general statistical usage, _____ or co-relation refers to the departure of two random variables from independence.

a. Median
b. Time series analysis
c. Heteroskedastic
d. Correlation

10. A _____ is the period of time between the initiation of any process of production and the completion of that process. Thus the _____ for ordering a new car from a manufacturer may be anywhere from 2 weeks to 6 months. In industry, _____ reduction is an important part of lean manufacturing.

a. Lead time
b. 33 Strategies of War
c. 1990 Clean Air Act
d. 28-hour day

11. _____ or Postponement is a concept in supply chain management where the manufacturing process starts by making a generic or family product that is later differentiated into a specific end-product. This is a widely used method, especially in industries with high demand uncertainty, and can be effectively used to address the final demand even if forecasts cannot be improved.

An example would be Benetton and their knitted sweaters that are initially all white, and then dyed into different colors only when the season/customer color preference/demand is known.

a. Delayed differentiation
b. Demand chain
c. Materials management
d. Supply-Chain Operations Reference

12. A _____ system is a manufacturing system in which there is some amount of flexibility that allows the system to react in the case of changes, whether predicted or unpredicted. This flexibility is generally considered to fall into two categories, which both contain numerous subcategories.

The first category, machine flexibility, covers the system's ability to be changed to produce new product types, and ability to change the order of operations executed on a part. The second category is called routing flexibility, which consists of the ability to use multiple machines to perform the same operation on a part, as well as the system's ability to absorb large-scale changes, such as in volume, capacity, or capability.

Chapter 13. Risk-Pooling Strategies to Reduce and Hedge Uncertainty

a. Homeworkers
b. Flexible manufacturing
c. Manufacturing resource planning
d. Jidoka

13. In queueing theory, _____ is the proportion of the system's resources which is used by the traffic which arrives at it. It should be strictly less than one for the system to function well. It is usually represented by the symbol ρ.
    a. A Stake in the Outcome
    b. A4e
    c. Utilization
    d. AAAI

14. A _____ is a computer program typically used to provide some form of artificial intelligence, which consists primarily of a set of rules about behavior. These rules, termed productions, are a basic representation found useful in AI planning, expert systems and action selection. A _____ provides the mechanism necessary to execute productions in order to achieve some goal for the system.
    a. 33 Strategies of War
    b. 28-hour day
    c. 1990 Clean Air Act
    d. Production System

Chapter 14. Revenue Management with Capacity Controls

1. _____ is the process of understanding, anticipating and influencing consumer behavior in order to maximize revenue or profits from a fixed, perishable resource This process was first discovered by Dr. Matt H. Keller. The challenge is to sell the right resources to the right customer at the right time for the right price.
   a. Business model design
   b. Gap analysis
   c. Business networking
   d. Yield management

2. The _____ captures an expanded spectrum of values and criteria for measuring organizational success: economic, ecological and social. With the ratification of the United Nations and ICLEI _____ standard for urban and community accounting in early 2007, this became the dominant approach to public sector full cost accounting. Similar UN standards apply to natural capital and human capital measurement to assist in measurements required by _____, e.g. the ecoBudget standard for reporting ecological footprint.
   a. Triple bottom line
   b. 1990 Clean Air Act
   c. 33 Strategies of War
   d. 28-hour day

3. In economics, _____ is the desire to own something and the ability to pay for it. The term _____ signifies the ability or the willingness to buy a particular commodity at a given point of time.
   a. 1990 Clean Air Act
   b. 33 Strategies of War
   c. Demand
   d. 28-hour day

4. _____ is the process of estimation in unknown situations. Prediction is a similar, but more general term. Both can refer to estimation of time series, cross-sectional or longitudinal data.
   a. Forecasting
   b. 28-hour day
   c. 33 Strategies of War
   d. 1990 Clean Air Act

5. The _____ model is a mathematical model in operations management and applied economics used to determine optimal inventory levels. It is (typically) characterized by fixed prices and uncertain demand. If the inventory level is q, each unit of demand above q is lost.

The standard _____ profit function is:

Chapter 14. Revenue Management with Capacity Controls

$$\text{[equation]}$$

where D is a random variable representing demand, each unit is sold for price p and purchased for price c, and E is the expectation operator. The solution to the optimal stocking quantity of the _____ is:

$$\text{[equation]}$$

where F^{-1} denotes the inverse cumulative distribution function of D.

a. Multiscale decision making
b. 28-hour day
c. Newsvendor
d. 1990 Clean Air Act

6. In the fields of science, engineering, industry and statistics, _____ is the degree of closeness of a measured or calculated quantity to its actual (true) value. _____ is closely related to precision, also called reproducibility or repeatability, the degree to which further measurements or calculations show the same or similar results. _____ indicates proximity to the true value, precision to the repeatability or reproducibility of the measurement

The results of calculations or a measurement can be accurate but not precise, precise but not accurate, neither, or both.

a. AAAI
b. A4e
c. A Stake in the Outcome
d. Accuracy

7. _____ is the activity of estimating the quantity of a product or service that consumers will purchase. _____ involves techniques including both informal methods, such as educated guesses, and quantitative methods, such as the use of historical sales data or current data from test markets. _____ may be used in making pricing decisions, in assessing future capacity requirements, or in making decisions on whether to enter a new market.

a. Profitability index
b. 28-hour day
c. 1990 Clean Air Act
d. Demand Forecasting

8. _____ is one of the managerial functions like planning, organizing, staffing and directing. It is an important function because it helps to check the errors and to take the corrective action so that deviation from standards are minimized and stated goals of the organization are achieved in desired manner. According to modern concepts, _____ is a foreseeing action whereas earlier concept of _____ was used only when errors were detected. _____ in management means setting standards, measuring actual performance and taking corrective action.
   a. Decision tree pruning
   b. Schedule of reinforcement
   c. Turnover
   d. Control

Chapter 15. Supply Chain Coordination

1. The _____ is an observed phenomenon in forecast-driven distribution channels. The concept has its roots in J Forrester's Industrial Dynamics (1961) and thus it is also known as the Forrester Effect. Since the oscillating demand magnification upstream a supply chain reminds someone of a cracking whip it became famous as the _____.
   a. Bullwhip effect
   b. 28-hour day
   c. 1990 Clean Air Act
   d. 33 Strategies of War

2. In economics and sociology, an _____ is any factor (financial or non-financial) that enables or motivates a particular course of action, or counts as a reason for preferring one choice to the alternatives. It is an expectation that encourages people to behave in a certain way. Since human beings are purposeful creatures, the study of _____ structures is central to the study of all economic activity (both in terms of individual decision-making and in terms of co-operation and competition within a larger institutional structure.)
   a. A4e
   b. A Stake in the Outcome
   c. Incentive
   d. AAAI

3. A _____ is the system of organizations, people, technology, activities, information and resources involved in moving a product or service from supplier to customer. _____ activities transform natural resources, raw materials and components into a finished product that is delivered to the end customer. In sophisticated _____ systems, used products may re-enter the _____ at any point where residual value is recyclable.
   a. Wholesalers
   b. Supply chain
   c. Drop shipping
   d. Packaging

4. _____ is the management of a network of interconnected businesses involved in the ultimate provision of product and service packages required by end customers (Harland, 1996.) _____ spans all movement and storage of raw materials, work-in-process inventory, and finished goods from point of origin to point of consumption (supply chain.)

The definition an American professional association put forward is that _____ encompasses the planning and management of all activities involved in sourcing, procurement, conversion, and logistics management activities.

   a. Packaging
   b. Supply chain management
   c. Freight forwarder
   d. Drop shipping

Chapter 15. Supply Chain Coordination

5. Procter is a surname, and may also refer to:

    - Bryan Waller Procter (pseud. Barry Cornwall), English poet
    - Goodwin Procter, American law firm
    - _____, consumer products multinational

   a. Downstream
   b. Master and Servant Acts
   c. Strict liability
   d. Procter ' Gamble

6. In economics, _____ is the desire to own something and the ability to pay for it. The term _____ signifies the ability or the willingness to buy a particular commodity at a given point of time.
   a. 28-hour day
   b. 1990 Clean Air Act
   c. 33 Strategies of War
   d. Demand

7. A _____ is typically described as a deliberate plan of action to guide decisions and achieve rational outcome(s.) However, the term may also be used to denote what is actually done, even though it is unplanned.

The term may apply to government, private sector organizations and groups, and individuals.

   a. 28-hour day
   b. 33 Strategies of War
   c. Policy
   d. 1990 Clean Air Act

8. In economics, business, retail, and accounting, a _____ is the value of money that has been used up to produce something, and hence is not available for use anymore. In economics, a _____ is an alternative that is given up as a result of a decision. In business, the _____ may be one of acquisition, in which case the amount of money expended to acquire it is counted as _____.
   a. Cost overrun
   b. Fixed costs
   c. Cost allocation
   d. Cost

Chapter 15. Supply Chain Coordination

9. _____ exists when sales of identical goods or services are transacted at different prices from the same provider. In a theoretical market with perfect information, no transaction costs or prohibition on secondary exchange (or re-selling) to prevent arbitrage, _____ can only be a feature of monopoly and oligopoly markets, where market power can be exercised. Otherwise, the moment the seller tries to sell the same good at different prices, the buyer at the lower price can arbitrage by selling to the consumer buying at the higher price but with a tiny discount.

   a. Pricing objectives
   b. Price points
   c. Target costing
   d. Price discrimination

10. _____ is a broad label that refers to any individuals or households that use goods and services generated within the economy. The concept of a _____ is used in different contexts, so that the usage and significance of the term may vary.

Typically when business people and economists talk of _____s they are talking about person as _____, an aggregated commodity item with little individuality other than that expressed in the buy/not-buy decision.

   a. 1990 Clean Air Act
   b. Consumer
   c. 33 Strategies of War
   d. 28-hour day

11. _____ is a joint trade and industry body working towards making the grocery sector as a whole more responsive to consumer demand and promote the removal of unnecessary costs from the supply chain.

The _____ movement beginning in the mid-nineties was characterized by the emergence of new principles of collaborative management along the supply chain. It was understood that companies can serve consumers better, faster and at less cost by working together with trading partners.

   a. Entertainment Management
   b. Efficient Consumer Response
   c. Event management
   d. Exception management

12. In economics, _____ is a rise in the general level of prices of goods and services in an economy over a period of time. When the general price level rises, each unit of the functional currency buys fewer goods and services; consequently, _____ is a decline in the real value of money--a loss of purchasing power in the internal medium of exchange which is also the monetary unit of account in an economy. A chief measure of general price-level _____ is the general _____ rate, which is the percentage change in a general price index (normally the Consumer Price Index) over time.

a. A4e
b. Inflation
c. Economy
d. A Stake in the Outcome

13. _____ is a concept that aims to enhance supply chain integration by supporting and assisting joint practices. _____ seeks cooperative management of inventory through joint visibility and replenishment of products throughout the supply chain. Information shared between suppliers and retailers aids in planning and satisfying customer demands through a supportive system of shared information.
    a. Career portfolios
    b. Collaborative Planning, Forecasting and Replenishment
    c. Groups decision making
    d. Timesheets

14. _____ refers to the structured transmission of data between organizations by electronic means. It is used to transfer electronic documents from one computer system to another (ie) from one trading partner to another trading partner. It is more than mere E-mail; for instance, organizations might replace bills of lading and even checks with appropriate _____ messages.
    a. A Stake in the Outcome
    b. A4e
    c. AAAI
    d. Electronic data interchange

15. _____ is the process of estimation in unknown situations. Prediction is a similar, but more general term. Both can refer to estimation of time series, cross-sectional or longitudinal data.
    a. 1990 Clean Air Act
    b. 33 Strategies of War
    c. 28-hour day
    d. Forecasting

16. In decision theory and estimation theory, the _____ of an estimator, $\hat{\theta}$, of an unknown parameter of the distribution, θ, is the expected value of the loss function

$$R(\theta, \hat{\theta}) = \mathbb{E}_\theta L(\theta, \hat{\theta}) = \int L(\theta, \hat{\theta}) \, dP_\theta.$$

Chapter 15. Supply Chain Coordination

where dP_θ is a probability measure parametrized by θ.

- For a scalar parameter θ and a quadratic loss function,

$$L(\theta, \hat{\theta}) = (\theta - \hat{\theta})^2$$

the _____ function becomes the mean squared error of the estimate,

$$R(\theta, \hat{\theta}) = E_\theta(\theta - \hat{\theta})^2$$

- In density estimation, the unknown parameter is probability density itself. The loss function is typically chosen to be a norm in an appropriate function space. For example, for L^2 norm,

$$L(f, \hat{f}) = \|f - \hat{f}\|_2^2$$

the _____ function becomes the mean integrated squared error

$$R(f, \hat{f}) = E\|f - \hat{f}\|^2$$

a. Financial modeling
b. Linear model
c. Risk aversion
d. Risk

17. _____ is a family of business models in which the buyer of a product provides certain information to a supplier of that product and the supplier takes full responsibility for maintaining an agreed inventory of the material, usually at the buyer's consumption location (usually a store.) A third party logistics provider can also be involved to make sure that the buyer has the required level of inventory by adjusting the demand and supply gaps.

As a symbiotic relationship, _____ makes it less likely that a business will unintentionally become out of stock of a good and reduces inventory in the supply chain.

a. Supply Chain Risk Management
b. Supply-Chain Operations Reference
c. Delayed differentiation
d. Vendor managed inventory

Chapter 15. Supply Chain Coordination

18. In probability theory, a probability distribution is called _____ if its cumulative distribution function is _____. This is equivalent to saying that for random variables X with the distribution in question, Pr[X = a] = 0 for all real numbers a, i.e.: the probability that X attains the value a is zero, for any number a. If the distribution of X is _____ then X is called a _____ random variable.
   a. Continuous
   b. Pay Band
   c. Decision tree pruning
   d. Connectionist expert systems

19. _____ is the process of understanding, anticipating and influencing consumer behavior in order to maximize revenue or profits from a fixed, perishable resource This process was first discovered by Dr. Matt H. Keller. The challenge is to sell the right resources to the right customer at the right time for the right price.
   a. Business networking
   b. Gap analysis
   c. Business model design
   d. Yield management

20. In economics and finance, _____ is the change in total cost that arises when the quantity produced changes by one unit. It is the cost of producing one more unit of a good. Mathematically, the _____ function is expressed as the first derivative of the total cost (TC) function with respect to quantity (Q.)
   a. Cost overrun
   b. Variable cost
   c. Transaction cost
   d. Marginal cost

21. _____ is one of the four Ps of the marketing mix. The other three aspects are product, promotion, and place. It is also a key variable in microeconomic price allocation theory.
   a. Penetration pricing
   b. Price floor
   c. Transfer pricing
   d. Pricing

22. In sociology, _____ is the social process of becoming or being made marginal (to relegate or confine to a lower social standing or outer limit or edge, as of social standing); 'the _____ of the underclass'; '_____ of literature' and many other are some examples. _____ involves people being denied degrees of power. _____ has the potential to result in severe material deprivation, and in its most extreme form can exterminate groups.

a. Social network analysis
b. Role conflict
c. Soft skill
d. Marginalization

23. In finance, an _____ is a contract between a buyer and a seller that gives the buyer the right--but not the obligation--to buy or to sell a particular asset (the underlying asset) at a later day at an agreed price. In return for granting the _____, the seller collects a payment (the premium) from the buyer. A call _____ gives the buyer the right to buy the underlying asset; a put _____ gives the buyer of the _____ the right to sell the underlying asset.

a. A Stake in the Outcome
b. Option
c. A4e
d. AAAI

24. A _____ is a computer program typically used to provide some form of artificial intelligence, which consists primarily of a set of rules about behavior. These rules, termed productions, are a basic representation found useful in AI planning, expert systems and action selection. A _____ provides the mechanism necessary to execute productions in order to achieve some goal for the system.

a. 1990 Clean Air Act
b. 28-hour day
c. 33 Strategies of War
d. Production System

25. In probability theory and statistics, the _____ is a normalized measure of dispersion of a probability distribution. It is defined as the ratio of the standard deviation σ to the mean μ:

$$c_v = \frac{\sigma}{\mu}$$

This is only defined for non-zero mean, and is most useful for variables that are always positive. It is also known as unitized risk.

a. Control chart
b. Failure rate
c. Frequency distribution
d. Coefficient of variation

26. In probability theory and statistics, the _____ of a random variable is the integral of the random variable with respect to its probability measure. For discrete random variables this is equivalent to the probability-weighted sum of the possible values, and for continuous random variables with a density function it is the probability density-weighted integral of the possible values.
   a. A Stake in the Outcome
   b. AAAI
   c. A4e
   d. Expected value

27. In mathematics, _____ are used in the study of chance and probability. They were developed to assist in the analysis of games of chance, stochastic events, and the results of scientific experiments by capturing only the mathematical properties necessary to answer probabilistic questions. Further formalizations have firmly grounded the entity in the theoretical domains of mathematics by making use of measure theory.
   a. Correlation
   b. Random variables
   c. Median
   d. Time series

28. In probability theory and statistics, _____ is a measure of the variability or dispersion of a population, a data set, or a probability distribution. A low _____ indicates that the data points tend to be very close to the same value (the mean), while high _____ indicates that the data are 'spread out' over a large range of values.

For example, the average height for adult men in the United States is about 70 inches (178 cm), with a _____ of around 3 in (8 cm.)

   a. Failure rate
   b. Normal distribution
   c. Standard deviation
   d. Frequency distribution

29. _____ is a mathematical science pertaining to the collection, analysis, interpretation or explanation, and presentation of data. It also provides tools for prediction and forecasting based on data. It is applicable to a wide variety of academic disciplines, from the natural and social sciences to the humanities, government and business.
   a. Simple moving average
   b. Location parameter
   c. Failure rate
   d. Statistics

30. _____ is one of the four elements of marketing mix. An organization or set of organizations (go-betweens) involved in the process of making a product or service available for use or consumption by a consumer or business user.

The other three parts of the marketing mix are product, pricing, and promotion.

a. Matching theory
b. Missing completely at random
c. Job creation programs
d. Distribution

31. In probability theory and statistics, the _____ or Gaussian distribution is a continuous probability distribution that describes data that clusters around a mean or average. The graph of the associated probability density function is bell-shaped, with a peak at the mean, and is known as the Gaussian function or bell curve.

The _____ can be used to describe, at least approximately, any variable that tends to cluster around the mean.

a. Histogram
b. Heteroskedastic
c. Generalized normal distribution
d. Normal distribution

32. In probability theory and statistics, a _____ identifies either the probability of each value of an unidentified random variable (when the variable is discrete), or the probability of the value falling within a particular interval (when the variable is continuous.) The _____ describes the range of possible values that a random variable can attain and the probability that the value of the random variable is within any (measurable) subset of that range. The Normal distribution, often called the 'bell curve'

When the random variable takes values in the set of real numbers, the _____ is completely described by the cumulative distribution function, whose value at each real x is the probability that the random variable is smaller than or equal to x.

a. Frequency distribution
b. Probability distribution
c. Statistically significant
d. Median

Chapter 15. Supply Chain Coordination

33. A _____ is a list of the general tasks and responsibilities of a position. Typically, it also includes to whom the position reports, specifications such as the qualifications needed by the person in the job, salary range for the position, etc. A _____ is usually developed by conducting a job analysis, which includes examining the tasks and sequences of tasks necessary to perform the job.

   a. Recruitment
   b. Recruitment Process Insourcing
   c. Recruitment advertising
   d. Job description

34. In probability theory and statistics, the _____s are a class of continuous probability distributions. They describe the times between events in a Poisson process, i.e. a process in which events occur continuously and independently at a constant average rate.

The probability density function (pdf) of an _____ is

Here >λ > 0 is the parameter of the distribution, often called the rate parameter.

   a. A Stake in the Outcome
   b. AAAI
   c. A4e
   d. Exponential distribution

35. In statistics, decision theory and economics, a _____ is a function that maps an event (technically an element of a sample space) onto a real number representing the economic cost or regret associated with the event.

Less technically, in statistics a _____ represents the loss (cost in money or loss in utility in some other sense) associated with an estimate being 'wrong' (different from either a desired or a true value) as a function of a measure of the degree of wrongness (generally the difference between the estimated value and the true or desired value.)

Both Frequentist and Bayesian statistical theory involve calculating statistics in such a way as to minimize the expected loss observed from being wrong given a set of assumptions about the data and one's _____.

   a. 1990 Clean Air Act
   b. Loss function
   c. 33 Strategies of War
   d. 28-hour day

36. _____ is a way of expressing knowledge or belief that an event will occur or has occurred. In mathematics the concept has been given an exact meaning in _____ theory, that is used extensively in such areas of study as mathematics, statistics, finance, gambling, science, and philosophy to draw conclusions about the likelihood of potential events and the underlying mechanics of complex systems.

The word _____ does not have a consistent direct definition.

a. Time series analysis
b. Statistics
c. Probability
d. Standard deviation

37. The _____ model is a mathematical model in operations management and applied economics used to determine optimal inventory levels. It is (typically) characterized by fixed prices and uncertain demand. If the inventory level is q, each unit of demand above q is lost.

The standard _____ profit function is:

where D is a random variable representing demand, each unit is sold for price p and purchased for price c, and E is the expectation operator. The solution to the optimal stocking quantity of the _____ is:

where F^{-1} denotes the inverse cumulative distribution function of D.

a. 1990 Clean Air Act
b. Newsvendor
c. 28-hour day
d. Multiscale decision making

38. In queueing theory, _____ is the proportion of the system's resources which is used by the traffic which arrives at it. It should be strictly less than one for the system to function well. It is usually represented by the symbol ρ.
a. AAAI
b. Utilization
c. A Stake in the Outcome
d. A4e

ANSWER KEY

Chapter 1
1. d 2. b 3. d 4. d 5. d 6. d 7. d 8. c 9. d 10. b
11. d 12. d 13. d 14. d

Chapter 2
1. d 2. b

Chapter 3
1. a 2. a 3. b 4. d 5. a 6. b

Chapter 4
1. d 2. d 3. c 4. d 5. c 6. d 7. a 8. d 9. b 10. d
11. c

Chapter 5
1. d 2. d 3. d 4. d 5. d 6. b 7. b 8. d 9. d 10. a

Chapter 6
1. d 2. d 3. a 4. d 5. b 6. d 7. b 8. b 9. d 10. a
11. a 12. d 13. d 14. d 15. d 16. c 17. c 18. d 19. d

Chapter 7
1. d 2. d 3. d 4. b 5. c 6. d

Chapter 8
1. d 2. d 3. d 4. d 5. d 6. a 7. d 8. d 9. a 10. c
11. d 12. d 13. a 14. d 15. c 16. d

Chapter 9
1. d 2. d 3. a 4. d 5. c 6. d 7. d 8. d 9. b 10. b
11. d 12. d 13. d 14. d 15. c 16. d 17. a 18. c 19. d 20. b

Chapter 10
1. c 2. d 3. b 4. a 5. c 6. c 7. a 8. b 9. b 10. d
11. a 12. a 13. d 14. d 15. c 16. a 17. a 18. a

Chapter 11
1. d 2. d 3. d 4. d 5. d 6. d

Chapter 12
1. a 2. d 3. a 4. a 5. d 6. d 7. a 8. d 9. d 10. d
11. d 12. d 13. d 14. d 15. d 16. c 17. d 18. d 19. d 20. d

ANSWER KEY

Chapter 13
1. b   2. d   3. d   4. d   5. c   6. a   7. b   8. c   9. d   10. a
11. a   12. b   13. c   14. d

Chapter 14
1. d   2. a   3. c   4. a   5. c   6. d   7. d   8. d

Chapter 15
1. a   2. c   3. b   4. b   5. d   6. d   7. c   8. d   9. d   10. b
11. b   12. b   13. b   14. d   15. d   16. d   17. d   18. a   19. d   20. d
21. d   22. d   23. b   24. d   25. d   26. d   27. b   28. c   29. d   30. d
31. d   32. b   33. d   34. d   35. b   36. c   37. b   38. b

www.ingramcontent.com/pod-product-compliance
Lightning Source LLC
Chambersburg PA
CBHW081849230426
43669CB00018B/2882